WORDS IN TRANSIT

MY LOVE FOR THIS COUNTRY IS UNCONDITIONAL. BECAUSE OF WHAT IT STANDS FO

EL AMERICAN. I FEEL LIKE I AM FROM HERE. JUST WITHOUT THE DOCUMENTS

AT THE SAME TIME, I WAS SAYING THAT I'M AN INTELLECTUAL

Collected, Recorded, and Edited by Cathleen O'Keefe, Tema Silk, and John Voci for New England Public Radio

DISTRIBUTED FOR NEW ENGLAND PUBLIC RADIO BY UNIVERSITY OF MASSACHUSETTS PRESS

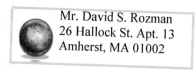

WORDS IN TRANSIT

STORIES OF IMMIGRANTS

Edited, with an Introduction, by Ilan Stavans   PHOTOGRAPHS BY BETH REYNOLDS

Published by New England Public Radio
Printed in the United States of America
Distributed by University of Massachusetts Press

ISBN 978-1-62534-219-5 (paperback)

Designed by Kristina Kachele Design, llc
Set in Alegreya Serif, Alegreya Sans, Bebas Neue
Printed and bound by Thomson-Shore, Inc.

CONTENTS

THE KATSURA TREE

Ilan Stavans

I lost two cities, lovely ones. And, vaster,
some realms I owned, two rivers, a continent.
I miss them, but it wasn't a disaster.
—Elizabeth Bishop, "One Art"

I remember vividly the day I arrived in the Pioneer Valley to settle down
and saw the spectacular Katsura tree for the first time. I had passed
through the region a number of times before, never thinking, even
remotely, that it would be the place where I would feel settled, the place
I would have the courage to call my own.

It was late August 1993. My wife, Alison, and my son, Joshua, were still
in New York City, where we lived. I had come to Amherst, Massachusetts,
on my own by car. We had rented a house on Orchard Street, but it wasn't
ready yet so I stayed for a while in a place not far from the Emily Dickinson
Homestead, which was just a few feet away from the railroad tracks. At
two in the morning, the train sped by on its way to Boston. The noise was
incredibly loud, waking me up like clockwork. That shaking sensation
was at once unpleasant and reassuring, for it reminded me of the endless

movement of New York City. In contrast, Amherst generally seemed full of trees and frighteningly quiet. That quiet made me uncomfortable. At night, it wouldn't let me sleep. I was thinking I had made a mistake in coming here.

You see, I not only came from New York, but I'm a city boy, born and bred. I am from Mexico City, one of the largest cities in the world, which in my teenage years during the seventies, was already a tumultuous place overwhelmed with people, air pollution, and traffic. I don't know if I ever came to love my city; I guess at some point I became used to it. In my late teens, I started dreaming of becoming a writer, and I wrote a novel—still unpublished, mercifully—that took place downtown in and around the Basílica de Guadalupe, the largest (at least until then) Catholic church in the Americas. While drafting it, I remember being struck by not quite having a sense of belonging, feeling that Mexico City was the place that I happened to be in, where I accidentally was born. I just couldn't find a way to be grounded. In fact, I was envious of others—my father, for instance— who seemed to know the city like the palm of their hand.

It took me some time to understand that this detachment, this sense of alienation, was an asset I could use to my advantage, that it was the traction I needed to step off on my own, to find another place where I could connect. I realized that my rootlessness was indeed part of the way I under- stood the world and that it perhaps comes from my condition of being a grandchild of immigrants. They were Yiddish-speaking *shtetl* dwellers who arrived in Mexico in the early decades of the twentieth century. They were welcomed, and in time they prospered, but the sense of being alien—not quite Mexican—was part of the education I received.

Before coming to the Pioneer Valley, I had spent time in Europe, in the Middle East and North Africa, and in Latin America. And then I moved to New York City. When I arrived there, the fact that everyone seemed to be passing by and on the go was comforting to me—to the point of making me think it was the right place to spend the rest of my life. I still nurture enormous love for the city and can't seem to spend a week without a deep desire to return, which I do regularly. But no sooner do I arrive than I want to finish my affairs for the day and leave again. It has become a place to visit, not a place to be.

The Pioneer Valley fits the definition of a place to be. At some point I had come here to visit the Yiddish Book Center, which struck me as a miraculous institution devoted to rescuing Yiddish culture, located just where it should be: the middle of nowhere. I had also visited the Emily Dickinson Homestead, not because I admired her poetry—it would literally take me years to reach that point of comfort—but because I saw her as the purest, most-pristine of American poets and wanted to see the place, the environment, in which she had created. In retrospect, I see that whenever I passed through the area, I left with a feeling of inner peace. Yet I wasn't in a period of my life in which peace was what I was looking for. I was in my twenties, and I was in search mode, testing myself, looking to find a bridge between my dreams and the world around me. The Valley didn't strike me as the place where one could "make it"; there was something flaccid about it.

Then, almost against all odds, I took a job at Amherst College. I was to begin teaching in a few weeks. The moment I arrived, I realized the place seemed beautiful to me. Not that I fully comprehended its qualities. For instance, only vaguely did I know that *Pioneer Valley* is the name given to the Massachusetts portion of the Connecticut River Valley. This small region includes three counties, Hamden, Hampshire, and Franklin, and it features four cities, Springfield, Holyoke, Northampton, and Greenfield. In other words, I didn't really know—internally, that is—that this place is a valley with its own metabolism. It took me a while, maybe a decade, to assimilate fully the geographic boundaries that surrounded the Valley, in part because I like to explore my environment the way an onion is built, layer by layer, and in part because my sense of direction is atrocious. Those first days, even the first weeks, I lived in complete disorientation. I got lost every time I left the apartment I rented. Much more than in New York City, blocks in the Valley resembled each other. At the same time, I had never seen such variety in a place—it was full of trees and ponds and bicycle paths—yet I couldn't map it in my mind. To this day, in my third decade in the area, I still have trouble identifying where south is. (The south is Mexico.)

My wife and son finally joined me as the semester was about to start and not long before the house we were scheduled to rent was ready. It is a house I adored from the moment I saw it. Designed in the Queen Anne style, the house was originally built in 1905. When we visited it for the first time, I felt the walls distilling endless joy, and as we started placing our things in the rooms, my wife and I were overwhelmed by a hunger to know as much about the house as possible. Shortly after moving in, a friend of ours who worked at the Jones Library gave us a series of news clippings about the property when it was built. And by happenstance, a couple of months later, an old man from Arizona knocked at the door. (I was away at the college, so I missed him.) My wife answered. The man said he was a geologist and the son of the original owner. He had come to town for some kind of professional meeting and wondered if he could see the place. Soon he started telling Alison all about the house's history: it cost his father $5,000 to build; it was a wedding present for his wife; the neighborhood was once an orchard; the visitor's grandmother had died in one of the rooms on the second floor; there had been chicken pens in the back yard at various points; wine and conserves were stored in the basement during winters; and other bits and pieces.

I learned from Alison all about the geologist's stories that afternoon when I came back from teaching. The visit immediately redefined our relationship with the place: We were no longer tenants (at the time we were only renting the place). Now the house was a theater and we were among its cast of characters. This new situation meant that we lived in conversation with our predecessors and that at some point, future tenants would be in conversations with us as well.

The visitor from Arizona also talked to my wife about his father. He was a paleontologist who unearthed many fossils. His name was Frederic Brewster Loomis. He had been born in Brooklyn, New York, in 1873, was educated at Amherst College, and received a doctorate from the Ludwig Maximilian University in Munich, Germany. He taught anatomy and was named professor of geology in 1917. His explorations took him as far as Patagonia. Scores of items he collected over the years are stored at the Beneski Museum of Natural History at Amherst and also at the Springfield Science Museum in Springfield, Massachusetts. For a while I was under the impression that Professor Loomis had disappeared on one of his expeditions and was never heard from again, but I later found out that he actually died in 1937, at the age of sixty-four, when on a trip to Alaska with his wife and son. He suffered a brain hemorrhage. He is buried at the Wildwood

Cemetery in Amherst, across the street from the elementary school my sons Joshua and Isaiah attended. He was the first person to import Bermuda onions to the United States. Apparently, he also donated a marble statue of Mary to the Catholic church in town.

It was the man from Arizona who made me feel that the Pioneer Valley has a gravitational force, that it is connected in subtle yet emphatic ways with many parts of the world. The man also called our attention to the Katsura tree. Of course, its imposing presence in the house's backyard was impossible to miss from the moment we arrived. And while it was a tree like no other, we had countless other things to pay attention to. In time I learned that its scientific name is *Cercidiphyllum japonicum*. It is 150 feet high and produces spurs along its twigs. Its leaves are around four inches long and about three inches wide. Its small, nutlike flowers come out in early spring and are pollinated by the wind. The fruit of those flowers is hard. It appears to be made of small pods; inside, there are numerous small, flat seeds, which become leaves in a matter of weeks. Every spring those leaves decorate our spirit, building a large cupola, and every autumn that cupola religiously sheds them in an equally short period of time. Truth is, the change happens in the blink of an eye. The ground is suddenly carpeted with leaves of astonishing yellows—not like the yellow from the oak trees but softer, more-subtle—and it has a wonderful aroma at the time. It takes a long time to rake them. During the winter, the tree looks desolate, lonely, absolutely naked, like a spindly ghost. Then comes spring again and the cycle begins anew, the branches regenerating themselves as if by magic. It is a spectacle to behold.

This astounding transformation often makes me want to talk to the Katsura tree. I feel like asking where its strength comes from and if its sturdiness will last forever. About the time of the visitor's arrival, I remember finding out that the tree is rare not only in the region but in the United States. It was brought to Amherst from the Far East by another member of the college faculty. There were originally ten specimens, but with the passing of time, not only have they grown enormously but offspring have popped up as well. In our own backyard there are several of them. Seeing these progeny moves me deeply. And what also affects me is the fact that some of the roots aren't quite underground; they run along the surface and can be seen by anyone passing by. I like this because the Katsura tree, also a transplant, seems to wear its ancestry on its sleeves, without shame, telling everybody that being strongly tied to the ground gives it the traction it needs to grow up to the sky, and that seeing traces of those ties is valuable to everyone.

Those exposed roots are a lesson to me as an immigrant. They make me think of my Mexican accent. I'm proud to say that I've never been ashamed of it. In fact, now that I have lived more time in the United States than outside it, I don't want to lose the tones of my first language. It speaks to my origins. My accent is like the roots of the Katsura tree showing through the soil.

Needless to say, the Pioneer Valley hasn't always welcomed immigrants. At times, it has actually made their lives miserable. Among my early delights after arriving in the region was to walk the streets of Northampton, a quaint city that gave me the impression of being almost in the margins of time, away from the frenzy of contemporary events, its inhabitants radiating conviviality. But larger urban enclaves are thornier. For example, Holyoke, an ethnic community where I often ventured, features gorgeous urban architecture that contrasts with its troubled politics. Holyoke was once a thriving mill town, but its abandoned factories were a distressing site, and Puerto Ricans, attracted in waves in an early-twentieth-century migration, were imprisoned in poverty. I remember once overhearing a conversation in Fernández's, a restaurant in downtown Holyoke. A couple of Puerto Ricans talked about a newly arrived family from Senegal faring better than they were. The message was clear—outsiders aren't created equally in America.

Truth is, immigration is about upheaval. It is about abandonment and dislocation. I have built precious friendships with immigrants to the Pioneer Valley who have gone through moments of intense alienation and for whom the idea of the United States as a land of opportunity feels foreign and deceptive. I remember an occasion in which the director of the Emily Dickinson Homestead invited me to recite the poet's verses in Spanish translation at different locations in Amherst. The invitation was part of an event featuring Dickinson's oeuvre in multiple languages. I was part of a cadre of immigrants and other readers whose voice declared her global stature. I was an admirer, and I had always wanted to learn more about her and maybe even to translate her into my native language, but I had never thought of her plight as connected with the immigrant experience. That evening, as I recited Dickinson's "I'm nobody. Who are you?" in front of a large crowd, the poem all of a sudden became about my own ordeal as a newcomer to the region. Yes, I had been nobody when coming to the Pioneer Valley. All newcomers are, in one way or another.

> How dreary – to be – Somebody!
> How public – like a Frog –
> To tell one's name – the livelong June –
> To an admiring Bog!

Yet, being a somebody is what belonging is about. That is, it is all about finding a place called home. The Katsura tree, I tell guests to our house, is from Japan. It enlivens my life. I know it is alone, outside its element, though it has been my irreplaceable companion for over two decades. When I'm far away from home, thinking of it gives me assurance.

But when I invoke its exuberance in my mind, I also think of loss. Elizabeth Bishop, who was born in Worcester, Massachusetts, once wrote a beautiful villanelle called "One Art," in which she explores loss not as a handicap, a deficiency, but as an art. She states in it that "the art of losing isn't hard to master and that so many things seem born with the intent to be lost that their loss is no disaster." This conception is soothing to me.

Living in a valley, I know now, grants you a bizarre sense of security. The place is a kind of bastion, a circle protected by natural hills, with a center that is really nowhere yet that serves as a gravitational force. The fertility of these lands is miraculous: corn, strawberries, apples, and peaches readily grow. The change of seasons is dramatic, outwardly as well as inwardly. Winter can be severe, making people keep to themselves, whereas summer is hot and humid, inviting us all to shed our inhibitions.

I ask myself, after all these years, what the culture of the Pioneer Valley is about. I have trouble answering. I realize, obviously, that it was here, not too far from Cape Cod, from the Plymouth Plantation, where the encounter between Europeans and indigenous tribes took place in seventeenth-century Massachusetts. It was here, also, where the Puritans set down roots, with the architecture still reminiscent of those first settlers. And it was here, among other places, where Transcendentalism took hold as a philosophy (Emily Dickinson befriended Ralph Waldo Emerson, its most-eloquent spokesman), persuading followers that the human mind and the cosmos are mirrors of each other. Somehow, two large Valley industries, agriculture and education, which often conflict elsewhere, coexist rather harmoniously in innovative ways. The Connecticut River and an assortment of small tributaries glide by in the background. People talk of living next to the river, of crossing it, and of fearing it might overflow during the rainy season, or of how stolid, how defiant, it is in the dead of January. It was that river, I'm aware, that made these lands attractive to the English. Although communities today depend on other means of transportation—the Massachusetts Turnpike, I-91, and Routes 9, 116, and 202—there is still something bucolic about the entire Valley ecosystem.

Yet the landscape has changed enormously in the last hundred years, as modernity took hold. The Valley, I tell acquaintances, half-jokingly, is halfway from New York and Boston, although, in mindset, it is quite distant from both. Still, it feels truly global; what happens in the Valley—politically, culturally, socially, religiously, and ecologically—has repercussions the world over. Even while newcomers feel local quite rapidly, the true locals are, to put it bluntly, increasingly difficult to find, such has been the overwhelming invasion of outsiders to the region.

That invasion makes me feel at home. Mysteriously, everyone feels like an immigrant here, even those who don't come from outside the country but from elsewhere within it. Not too long ago, I taught at the Hampshire County Jail in Northampton. The course, Life Is a Dream, was about literature that confuses the real with the fantastic. Half of my students were from the five colleges in the area and half were "inside" students, inmates—all male—interested in furthering their education. The experience was transformative. As is the case in prisons elsewhere in the nation, the population is predominantly black or Latino, although in this case whites constituted about a third. For security reasons, all of us, including me as the teacher, were asked not to volunteer personal information; thus,

I know where my "outside" students, about half of whom were black or Latino, came from, but of the rest I only have a partial picture. Some were gang members from Holyoke. Others talked of Springfield with affection. One had been in the military. They spoke different languages. Still, it took me no time to realize, largely due to the written assignments, that everyone without exception, inside or outside, saw themselves as alien. We were all coinciding in a fenced, monitored classroom inside a correctional facility that happened to be in the Pioneer Valley. Yet the Valley was an accident, the place where people had come to school or where they had been put in jail.

Surprisingly, that feeling of alienation was good. It made everyone come together. In fact, I often thought of the fertile soil in the Pioneer Valley because there was among the students an intellectual fertility I was completely enthralled by.

One inevitably thinks of immigration as a disquieting event in life, but it can also be a fulfilling one. There are periods in life when we are about accumulation, and there are periods in which we need to get rid of things. Obviously, we aren't always in control of the two. The journey of immigrants is often unpredictable. It is about rupture, about chaos. Yet the newcomer also has the capacity to reinvent herself in a way that is redeeming. Not often do we have the chance to say, "I'll start from scratch," and that opportunity is granted, gracefully or otherwise, to immigrants, who not surprisingly are endowed with a substantial amount of energy and decisiveness. They know that creativity is their only redemption, that in order to survive they need to be entrepreneurial. The United States is in a constant state of renewal precisely because its doors have always been open to newcomers. Yes, the anti-immigrant rhetoric is toxic, but it is not new. In truth, it is older than the country itself. That anti-immigrant feeling makes immigrants strong, more assertive. To succeed, they know they must beat the odds.

Words in Transit gathers a range of stories of immigrants, twenty-eight in all. The endeavor started in a conversation with my friend John Voci, Executive Director of Programing and Content at New England Public Radio. I suggested we form a team to collect oral histories of newcomers from around the globe to the Pioneer Valley. Amherst College was then immersed in a year-long colloquium on translation—also titled *Words in Transit*—seen in multiple perspectives: diplomacy, medical research, psychology, journalism, pedagogy, anthropology, and literature and the arts.

NEPR producer, Tema Silk, was the managing director for the project, whose objective was to identify and collect a range of voices—diverse and miscellaneous in their age and gender. Silk was responsible for locating and interviewing immigrants from as a wide a geographic area—from Hartford, Connecticut, to Worcester, Massachusetts—as possible. Their voices were captured by sound engineer Cathleen O'Keefe.

It was clear from the start that this wasn't an exercise in social science. The personal narratives recorded and assembled were not intended to be representative. In other words, serendipity, which arguably is the most distinctive feature of our universe, reigns free in these pages. In abbreviated form, many of the stories aired in *Morning Edition* accompanied on the NEPR website with the stunning photographic profiles by Beth Reynolds and others. They were greeted enthusiastically by viewers. This volume is an invitation to look at the community of newcomers as a whole, to listen to them with one's eyes, to look deeper into how immigration fortifies the texture of our cultural ecology.

I called the enterprise "words in transit" because to me it is all about languages on the move and the cultures they emerge from. To invoke Dickinson's lines again, we immigrants in our trek are nobodies in search of other nobodies. Since speaking about the experience might be fraught as well as empowering, the effort is about becoming a somebody. In turn, Elizabeth Bishop talks in her poem about losing a set of keys, a house, a river, a city, a continent—all these normal occurrences in a lifetime. But we aren't only made of loss. We are also made of gains. When we relocate, we may add a set of house keys, a river, a city . . .

We may also add a tree.

STARTING OVER

Tema Silk

This is a book about leaving a familiar place—whether you want to go or not—and starting over in an entirely new one—whether you are welcome or prepared, whether you fit in, or not. It's about the things, such as cups of Barry tea, that can help people remain attached to parts of their past they still yearn for. And it's about the gestures and kindnesses and discoveries that lead, sometimes sooner, sometimes later, to a sense of belonging here in this country. It's about choosing life over death, action over paralysis—it's about grit, determination, frustration, loss, success, and counting one's blessings.

The details in the stories that follow have much to teach us. One young man describes that on crossing the border, he hid in the trunk with total strangers as they encountered various checkpoints. And one young woman recalls the intense cold of the desert at night and the terrifying howls of the nearby animals as she clutched her mother's hand and walked silently into America.

A grown woman suddenly remembers shampooing her hair in the Mekong River as a very young girl. She sobs at the memory of the beauty of the water, the same river she would cross in the darkness of the following evening, with her mother's hand clamped over her little mouth and quiet, strong voice urging her to be silent lest they be shot.

Another young man, expressing sadness that was palpable, told us about waking up on a cold November morning—the first morning of his first day in America—walking outside, and standing on the sidewalk—just standing there, doing nothing more—for hours, unsure about where he was or what to do until a stranger asked him if he was alright and helped him back to his apartment.

Culture shock means something quite different to me now.

Other gems come from asides and reflections. A woman who has lived here for decades says about leaving Romania during dictator Nicolae Ceaușescu's reign: "My love for this country is unconditional. Because of what it stands for and what I found here. And I could just *never* take this for granted. What a *gift* this is and has been."

"There's a time when I felt like the world had fallen in on me," another man says about his harrowing and repeated tangles with danger and loneliness and hardship after escaping Burundi at the age of eleven, without his parents, but with his two younger sisters in tow. "There's a time I questioned whether God existed. There's a time I asked, 'What have I done to deserve this?' But human beings are resilient people. As soon as I realized that I could hang on another day, I challenged myself not to sit down licking my own wounds. I stood up, and then I said, 'No, I deserve better. I don't want to keep feeling sorry for myself.' Things really changed."

A painter and art instructor, who succeeded in becoming as respected for his artwork here in America as he had been in Africa, said he offers others in his shoes this advice: "When you come to America, you can be a great person if you want, and you can be a lower person if you want. It all depends on you. Sometimes you have to forget a little bit of the past. But this past has to be your backbone. To support you. Don't forget who you are. What you went through is the experience of your life. So this experience can be sold."

From these stories, we can also learn things about how we Americans are perceived by others. For the most part, we come off pretty well. Many immigrants mentioned our helpfulness and generosity. But there were also critical comments—about how much we take for granted the comfort in our lives, about the need to raise more resilient children and to respect education and experience obtained elsewhere, and about how we should learn more about the world outside of America and realize people in other societies we consider less developed can lead deeply satisfying and happy lives, sometimes happier lives than they can have here. These voices remind us that in other lands, the connection to family is more precious than here, that focusing on the individual as much as we do weakens us in some ways.

I came away from interviews deeply moved and deeply humbled, sorry for indignities people had endured in their homelands and sometimes here in America as well. And I was reminded—over and over—how much I have to be thankful for.

That includes the privilege I have had as manager of this project, with a formidably talented team.

Most importantly, I need to thank the people whose stories are in this book. I am grateful for their willingness to talk so openly about what it means to be an immigrant, a refugee, or someone without documentation living in this country. Often that meant delving into pasts rife with pain. Their accounts provide us with the chance to better understand them and, by extension, other people starting over here. And the more we understand, the stronger and more connected all of us will be.

IN A STRANGE NEW LAND

John Voci

A century ago, my grandparents came to this country from Italy and Lithuania as part of a great wave of immigration to the United States from Eastern and Western Europe. From the mid-nineteenth century to the early twentieth century, some fifty million people left their native countries for the United States. Like many, my grandparents came in search of a better life. They lived in immigrant communities in Worcester, Massachusetts, married, had families, and became part of this country and the American experience.

I wonder about my grandparents' lives and the circumstances of their passage to a new land. What source of strength guided them on their journey? What did they experience in their new country?

I know little about their early lives. As a teenager, my maternal grandmother traveled alone from her home in Vilnius, Lithuania, to Massachusetts. My maternal grandfather reputedly left Lithuania to avoid conscription in the Russian army. My paternal grandfather arrived in this country in 1904, one of approximately 193,000 Italians to immigrate to the United States that year. He adopted his new homeland by changing his name to James and, like that of many fellow immigrants, his adopted name was not his birth name. Three years later, my paternal grandmother arrived from her Calabrian village in Italy; she was already a widow at age seventeen.

Worcester was a city of immigrants living in three-decker homes in ethnic enclaves scattered throughout the city. Italians lived around Shrewsbury Street, Lithuanians on Vernon Hill, Irish and Poles near Kelly Square, and Swedes in Quinsigamond Village and Greendale. When I was growing up in the Worcester of the 1950s and 1960s, my grandparents were like those of my friends and schoolmates. Whether they were from Italy, Lithuania, Poland, Sweden, or Armenia, our grandparents spoke with heavy accents and in broken English. They represented a link to our ethnic heritage, but we knew little about their homeland or how and why they ended up in Worcester in the early years of the twentieth century.

The stories of those we interviewed for New England Public Radio's series *Words in Transit* are similar to those of my grandparents. The individuals we spoke with may have traveled here from Asia, Europe, Latin America, Africa, the Caribbean, and the Middle East, but their stories have themes similar to those of my grandparents: They came for a better life, because of opportunities, or to flee political oppression.

Words in Transit began as a radio and online initiative of New England Public Radio (NEPR) as part of Amherst College's Copeland Colloquium. Our goal was to bring the national conversation on immigration home to our community, to shift the discussion from an abstract debate around immigration policies to stories of individuals. It's one thing to have a policy discussion; it's something quite different to listen to harrowing accounts of fleeing from bullets and crossing the armed border at night, and to stories of settling in a strange new land.

Tema Silk was the *Words in Transit's* managing director; Cathleen O'Keefe, its producer; and I, its executive producer. We set out to collect interviews with a diverse group of individuals living in western New England. We sought people in communities throughout the station's listening area representing a broad cross section of age, class, gender, ethnicity, and nationality. Tema and our team of interns sought interviewees at community organizations, cultural centers, churches and synagogues, libraries, restaurants, and other public spaces. The hub of our region centered on the Pioneer Valley, but our reach extended to both central Massachusetts and northern Connecticut. We had contributions from immigrants living in the western Massachusetts counties of Hamden, Hampshire, and Franklin, and from others residing in central Massachusetts and in Hartford, Connecticut.

The majority of the interviews occurred at the NEPR studios in Amherst and Springfield with a few collected in recording facilities at Amherst College, Mount Holyoke College, and Capital Community College, and on location in homes and businesses. Tema conducted the interviews while Cathleen recorded them. For many interviewees, sitting in a sound studio in front of a microphone was a novel experience. Guiding the conversation, Tema sensitively drew out stories about our interviewees' home country, the factors that motivated their decision to leave, the experience of their journey, and their transition to a new land. In some cases, telling their stories was an emotional experience as participants recounted violence, loss, their families, and discrimination.

Editing the stories was one of the biggest challenges. We grappled with what to include, what to cut, and how best to convey someone's story. One of the hardest jobs fell to Cathleen. She had the responsibility of organizing and editing everyone's story into a succinct five- to ten-minute first-person narrative. Once the initial cut was complete, I worked on the final edit, often listening to each interview countless times for flow, continuity, and clarity. Many times, I came away from the process feeling that I had an intimate relationship with someone I had never met. The transcriptions that comprise this book are the words of our interviewees, complete with all the grammatical errors of a non-native speaker.

Thanks to Beth Reynolds's portraits and Pete Chilton's web design, the radio series came to life visually online at http://nepr.net/wordsintransit. Beth's photography was critical to the project as she skillfully captured our interviewees and their families in beautiful portraits, a process that required both sensitivity and care. Similar to the interview process, Beth had to gain the trust of her subjects; the stunning portraits are a testament to her art and skill. All the aural and visual elements came together thanks to Pete's design. His organization and presentation of the material helped to convey the narrative of our participants' stories. Now, thanks to the University of Massachusetts Press and the publication of this book, the stories and faces of this extraordinary group of individuals have a permanent physical home between these pages.

Working on this project was profoundly moving. It was an honor to meet the individuals portrayed in this collection and to hear and share their stories. I'm in awe of their courage, resilience, and optimism, and I hope that we've done them justice by conveying their stories honestly and accurately. I owe a tremendous debt to my grandparents for their sacrifice, and I wish that I had the opportunity as an adult to ask about their lives, about the experiences that shaped their arrival in this country, and about the dreams they had for their family.

In this collection we honor the people of all eras who have sacrificed to call this nation home.

ACKNOWLEDGMENTS

This compendium of oral histories with approximately twenty-eight immigrants in the Pioneer Valley, produced by New England Public Radio, was part of the year-long conversation at Amherst College devoted to translation in all walks of life, from politics to journalism, from literature to theater. The overall title was *Words in Transit*. The events took place during the academic year 2014–2015 and were sponsored by the Copeland Colloquium under the direction of Ilan Stavans. The project manager was Ryan Mihaly. Our wholehearted gratitude goes to the Copeland Fund for making the endeavor possible.

The overall success is due to many talented and devoted individuals who deserve tremendous thanks:

The interns were Leslie Coronel, Siyu Feng, Richard Park, Jessica Ramírez, Alexis Teyie, and Qi Xie. Special thanks to Catherine Choi, Rama Hagos, Hannah Thornton, and Caitlin Vanderberg.

From the community, Aliza Ansell, Holyoke Community College-Center for New Americans; Ted Barbour, Prosperity Candle, Easthampton; Alden Bourne; Michael Carolan, Clark University; Robert Chipkin; Susannah Crolius, Western Massachusetts Refugee and Immigrant Consortium; Taneisha Duggan, HartBeat Ensemble; Joanne Gold, Ludlow Adult Learning

Center; Magdalena Gómez, Teatro V!da; Gerry Harvey, Round the World Women; Robert Marmor, Jewish Family Service of Western Massachusetts; Ann Maggs and Victoria Maillo, Amherst College; Mohammed Najeeb, Services for New Americans, Ascentria Care Alliance; Steve Raider-Ginsberg, HartBeat Theater Ensemble; Lynne Weintraub, Jones Library; and Judy Wyman Kelly, West Hartford Human Rights Commission.

Special thanks to Nancy Caddigan, Intercultural Liaison, Hartford Public Library, whose boundless support included organizing a meeting with the Asylum Hill Neighborhood Association and scheduling interviews for most of our participants in Hartford, for whom the trip to Springfield was not possible. Also, to Emily Savin, who volunteered many hours of her time to energetically support the project in countless ways.

At Amherst College, thanks also to Jack Cheney, Catherine Ciepiela, John Drabinski, Liz Eddy, Catherine Epstein, Lauren Franks, John Kunhardt, Austin Sarat, and Janet Tobin.

And at NEPR, Pete Chilton, for his masterful web design; Vanessa Cerillo, for skillful promotion of the project; Sam Hudzik, for his thoughtful editing of the selections broadcast on NEPR; Joyce Skowyra for her contributions as a photographer and overall general support; Chris Daly; Georgette deFriesse; Fran Goodwin; and Pam Malumphy. Finally, we appreciate the support of Martin Miller, General Manager and CEO.

At University of Massachusetts Press, director Mary Dougherty embraced the book from the start. Sally Nichols and John Harrison provided essential advice, Tina Kachele adapted the contents into a superb interior design, and Durwood Ball did a magnificent copyediting job.

WORDS IN TRANSIT

I ALMOST LOST MY LIFE BEFORE I EVEN HAD THE CHANCE TO HAVE IT.

. YOU HAVE TO ALWAYS THINK OF YOURSELF, "YES, THERE'S A POSSIBILITY

WHAT WE CALLED IT IS THE "SECOND DEATH." STAYING IN SYR

"KNOWING WHERE YOU CAME FROM"

Sovann-Malis Loeung

Cambodia

I can only speak to what I was told, not to what I can remember. My mother hadn't really told us much, and that was very normal for our parents that had come from Cambodia—the war-torn genocide that happened—to not really speak on that experience. It's too painful, let's not remember that, it's too painful.

What I do know is basically of stories from my mom and her friends talking about how it was. Not necessarily connecting with me, but just reminiscing of how it was for them: "Your mother, while we were escaping Cambodia, she was carrying you, she was pregnant, and she fell down in the ditch, and somehow she crawled up with you in her belly, and she was really determined to be with us and continue on this journey of leaving Cambodia."

And that to me was very touching: Oh my God, you know, this woman did not let that deter her from leaving Cambodia. And not from the will that she wants to leave, but from the will that she has to for the safety of her kids. That was one indication that she was very strong.

We went from Cambodia to the Thai borders, where the refugee camps were, and we stayed there for—I'm not really quite sure how long, probably a year. But we stayed there for some time, and then we transitioned to the

An administrative assistant in the Education Department at the University of Massachusetts, Amherst, Sovann-Malis Loeung was two or three years old—she will never know which—when she escaped Cambodia with her mother. Over the years, her mother resisted giving her and her siblings detailed information about the episode, which remains foggy. Loeung does know her father died as they were leaving, but isn't sure how.

Philippines, and then to Long Beach, California. It was normal for refugees to be in another place first before they arrived to the United States.

I was part of a community that spoke Cambodian at the house, and also English outside the house. We lived in an apartment complex where most of us were Cambodian refugees. Our first home was in an apartment, and we lived with my uncle and his family in a one- or two-bedroom household. Everybody slept on the floor. And that was fine, you know? No complaints. Hey, we're in a place where we get to be with each other, we were used to sleeping on the floors anyways, we had clothes—and this is not to say that we didn't have clothes back in Cambodia, but it was just a transition of, OK, this is something new for us. We were happy with new things, even if it was used. I just remember having to go looking for cans, aluminum cans for recycling, to deposit them. And thinking to myself, Well, OK, this is OK, you know? This is a way that people can make money.

Having the feeling of being American wasn't really on my thoughts. It was just another place to stay for me. Because I had some disconnect with the country of Cambodia because I didn't remember that. We just never really talked about it much. We moved back and forth: when we got to California, we moved from California to Massachusetts, and the piece of having to assimilate didn't allow me to think about, Why is it that we left? But I do just remember having the differences in having the Cambodian language spoken at home, versus English outside and in school. The connection is important to me, because I feel that knowing where you came from, the history, is very much important, to be able to identify how you are with yourself. Not just only with yourself, but also to others.

Our family wasn't searching for the American dream: we were just escaping our country. I think there has to be a solid definition about the difference between immigration and being a refugee, where there's a push and pull factor—the United States being a pull factor of having the American dream. Being a refugee, the refugee experience is, Look, I didn't want to leave my country, but I have to—because of war, because of whatever that is. There's a push factor. The difference between the two has to be noted somewhere.

. . . KNOWING WHERE YOU CAME FROM, THE HISTORY, IS
VERY MUCH IMPORTANT, TO BE ABLE TO IDENTIFY HOW
YOU ARE WITH YOURSELF. NOT JUST ONLY WITH YOURSELF,
BUT ALSO TO OTHERS.

OUR FAMILY WASN'T SEARCHING FOR THE AMERICAN
DREAM: WE WERE JUST ESCAPING OUR COUNTRY.

I CAN ONLY SPEAK TO WHAT I WAS TOLD,
NOT TO WHAT I CAN REMEMBER.

ONCE I REVEAL TO SOMEBODY WHO'S AN
IMMIGRANT THAT I AM ALSO AN IMMIGRANT,
YOU CAN SEE THEIR BODY RELAX.

"YOU DON'T WANT TO STICK OUT"

Heather Neal
Ireland

Once I reveal to somebody who's an immigrant that I am also an immigrant, you can see their body relax. It takes the edge off. And it feels like you have somebody else who understands that everything here is just new or different. Despite the fact that I've been here thirty-something years.

We came here in 1979, and Ireland was going through a depression. My dad was here working as an artist. He got a job designing Irish pubs in Manhattan, and he got us green cards after he got his green card.

We moved from a place where I overlooked the ocean to an apartment on the lower floor of an apartment building. My dad was the super of the building. And I felt like I was the only white kid for miles. And it was definitely interesting. I had to acclimate very quickly. I started to lose my accent immediately because you know, if you stick out, you don't want to stick out and have a funny accent.

I was the type of kid that sort of just wandered around all day long during the summer, or after school, just me and the dog wandering around on the beaches and then through fields, and to then all of a sudden be in this very fast-paced, jam-packed environment with all these very mature girls who had very specific ideas about what you should look like and act like. . . . And one girl looked at the other girl and said, "Mira, look at her!"

A licensed massage therapist in Greenfield, Massachusetts, Heather Neal was born and raised in Ireland to British parents. She spent her adolescence in Spanish Harlem, where she found fitting in a challenge. Decades later, she still misses Ireland while also having a sense of belonging here in America.

9

And the other one looked at me and said, "Does your mother dress you?" And I answered "Yes," because she did! So it was. It was tough. It was tough trying to fit into that.

I miss Ireland. I until recently I had traveled back every year. And my parents retired back there, and so we would go over and take care of them. And they've since passed away. But we traveled back every year. So every year I got to fill my soul, and it would get filled the second I flew over and saw the patchwork of green, and I could walk on the cliffs and smell the air and the seaweed. And that has always helped me . . . cope here.

But recently I don't have that. So I find myself starting to cling to different things. And the one thing I did bring over and I keep is my tea.

While I still consider myself either British or Irish, if I was to identify as a lesbian I'd identify as an American lesbian.

Coming out here, I identified with a community, and it was a community of people from all over the world. You know, I had Peruvian friends and African friends and Canadian and French friends, but we were all lesbians. So that made me feel very much a part of this country, of that, that melting pot idea.

"THE LUCKIEST PERSON ON EARTH"

Veronica Vaida

Romania

I was asked to lead a delegation of Romanian officials from my hometown to Holland. So I prepared all the things necessary for this trip, and my director, which here translates into a principal of the high school, they were proud that I was chosen to go and lead the delegation. And just a couple of weeks before leaving, I was called to the police office and I was asked if I had relatives in the West—I had relatives in France, my mother's brother; by that time, I had relatives in Israel.

It would have been a very frightening thing, but the head of the police in this town was a gentleman. He explained that they cannot give me a passport to lead this delegation. And so I went home and I told my family that we are leaving.

They understood when I explained that forever we are going to be second-class citizens; we are not going to be able to get ahead, and even worse than that, our children will have no future. And with that, we proceeded and applied. [New York Senator] Jacob Javits, he found out that [Nicolae] Ceaușescu's Romania was not nice to minorities and to their Jews. And that the favored nation status which was given to Ceaușescu that meant a lot of money that Romania would get—which of course went into his Swiss bank account, we later found out—but nevertheless, Jews had no

Veronica Vaida first dreamed of escaping Communist-ruled Romania as a child. As a young adult with a degree in teaching, she experienced anti-Semitism firsthand. She immediately announced to her husband and two daughters it was time to leave. Through a series of coincidences, she managed to obtain visas for her family relatively quickly. Vaida eventually settled in West Hartford, where she teaches yoga at the Jewish Community Center.

MY LOVE FOR THIS COUNTRY IS UNCONDITIONAL. BECAUSE OF WHAT IT STANDS FOR AND WHAT I FOUND HERE.

freedom. Many Jews we knew, they were sitting on their luggage for many, many years, and they were kicked out of their jobs

What happened then, there was a blitzing of President [Richard] Nixon and [Secretary of State] Kissinger throughout all the Communist countries just as we applied, and they put Ceaușescu and some others—probably the Polish, the Hungarian leaders—on notice that this favored nation status will be taken away unless they respect human rights. Compared to other people, we were given in our hands our passports in eight months.

I questioned my education, my degree, whether I will ever be able to be an English teacher here, and am I coming to a country where English is not my mother tongue, who's going to allow me to teach? And that's when I said to myself that no matter what I'm gonna do, even if I'm gonna maybe clean houses, I don't know, I don't want to live there.

From Romania, the way to come to the West was through different way stations. There was one in Greece, so that's where we went. And from Greece, because my husband had a childhood friend in Montreal, Canada, and we had the choice between the United States and Canada, and we were tremendously scared off by the United States at that time, and because we—it seemed like we would not know anybody; and then in Canada we would—we opted for Montreal. And then after six years living in Montreal we wanted to come to the United States.

I came to New York, and I was basically offered a job as an activity therapist, working with mentally handicapped adults in a very difficult neighborhood in the south Bronx, where it was hard to get professionals to go and work there. And I worked there for six years, at the UCP, United Cerebral Palsy of New York State. And in my whole entire life it turned out to be the most meaningful job. I appreciated my family in a different way, my children. The affection that I received from those clients, we called

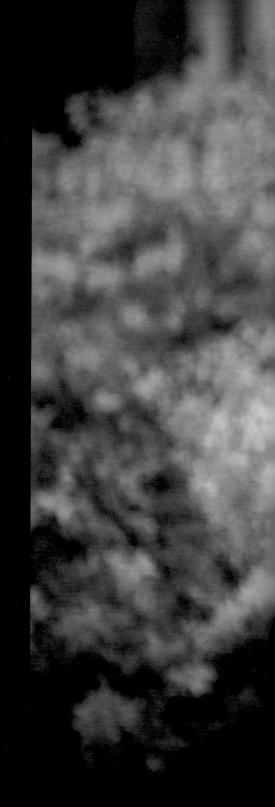

them, that I had in my class, cannot equal anything in my life since.

I am very grateful for my education, which turned out to be a lot better than what I thought it was, and I am grateful that it was appreciated—its value—here.

My love for this country is unconditional. Because of what it stands for and what I found here. And I could just never take this for granted. What a gift this is and has been. It just enabled me to teach my children that failure is not really an option.

I constantly kept pinching myself that I am here, that we are here. That I feel the luckiest person on earth, to be able to live here.

I AM VERY GRATEFUL FOR MY EDUCATION, WHICH TURNED
OUT TO BE A LOT BETTER THAN WHAT I THOUGHT IT WAS . . .

"I EXIST BECAUSE YOU EXIST"

Pascal Akimana
Burundi

I come from a country called Burundi where it was ravaged by civil war. I became a refugee at an early age, and I went to the neighboring country The Democratic Republic of Congo. I looked after my sister when I was eleven. My other sister was nine, another one was seven.

In 1993, they killed the first president who was elected democratically. That sparked the violence.

It was at night, the gunshots started. I heard gunshots all over in the village. People were screaming. And suddenly the neighbors were coming to our house, waking people, saying, "We are being killed! So and so is being hacked by machetes. And soldiers, military are there."

We started running. When I say "we," I mean the family. Like bullets are being [fired] all over. And the gunshots are all over. We can see the enemies. It wasn't dark, it was like five in the morning.

I took direction for the Congo with other people who were running for their lives. For safety . . .

When we reached the border of the Congo, the Congolese military were not so kind to us. They brutalized refugees and they started raping women and they stole from what the refugees had, what we had.

I witnessed those things.

Pascal Akimana fled Burundi at the age of eleven as his village was being attacked by rebels. He became separated from his parents at the Congolese border and took on the care of his two younger sisters. Narrowly escaping brutality and death time and time again in the ensuing years, Akimana finally found safety in South Africa, where he began his work as a humanitarian. Now living in Holyoke, Massachusetts, he recently earned his master's degree in peace building and conflict transformation. He is the president of the Massachusetts-based diaspora organization Engaging for Action in Burundi. He is also executive director of the nonprofit Umoja Now, which is committed to engaging Burundian men and boys to promote gender equality and decrease violence against women and girls.

Photo credit: Joyce Skowyra.

And there were some aid workers working for the UNHCR [United Nations High Commission on Refugees] and Red Cross in Congo who heard that there were refugees from Burundi who were stuck in the bush, and then when they received us, and they took those women who were raped to the clinic—there was a clinic run by the nuns—they took the refugees who had been brutally attacked by the Congolese military into that clinic and myself and my two sisters, with other crowd we were put in the refugee camp.

There was no bed. There was nothing, nothing at all.

Soon the cholera attacked because where you find so many people . . . and no bathrooms. There was no food. People were hungry. It took time and days, if not weeks, for us to get aid in terms of food and medical attention.

The local people who had received us, they were already getting burdened because refugees were going to their fields stealing food from the crops that they had planted, and they started attacking refugees and killing them. I saw all those things.

And that refugee camp in Congo was very hard. And I said: "I don't want to die here. I don't want to be killed by Congolese. Or even just be killed because I am hungry. I want food, I came to a country of safety, but I'm going to lose my life here."

I told my two sisters, "We should rather go back home than get killed; we don't even know where our dad is."

And they were very young. So I took them. . . . We walked about four or five hours—because that refugee camp was not too far from the border. And when we went there, we found my dad was there and his wife. They had run [a] different direction and they had come back as well.

. . . WE WERE PUT IN THE REFUGEE CAMP. THERE WAS NO BED. THERE WAS NOTHING, NOTHING AT ALL.

Burundi wasn't safe. I stayed with my sisters under hard conditions. My mom had gone to a different refugee camp, which was very far. There was no communication.

At my house, I had to work hard. I put myself in school because my dad was a really irresponsible man. I had to work hard to care for my siblings, and I put myself in school; I went to boarding school.

There was a program at the time that was receiving children who were orphans or who didn't have any means to put themselves, or their parents put them in schools. And then they transferred me to boarding school; it's in the coffee plantation.

And because it was in the coffee plantation in the bush, that's where the fighting between the rebels and the military were happening. I saw people being killed. Some of our professors were shot at. We were in the cafeteria one day eating and the bullets were flying. The woman who was the secretary of the school—she was burned alive in the car.

The military would bomb the rebels who were assumed to be in the coffee plantation, and that coffee plantation was at school. The military would accuse students of conspiring with the rebels to attack the military. And some rebels, when they don't see you working with them—because they would come to the school spying—they will think you were conspiring with the government military.

And one night, the rebels came, they wanted to recruit new rebels. They opened the dormitory and there were bullets all over. The government had deployed some military camp so they could guard the students.

When the rebels came, they fought with those soldiers. The soldiers, they ran. And then the rebels took some students and the headmaster and some of the teachers into the bush.

I was lucky. I fled because I was little. It was in the dark. I hid in the bush. I ran with the other students. We find ourselves in Muyinga. And Muyinga is another province that is close to Tanzania. That's how I left Burundi!

This time in the refugee camp in Tanzania, life wasn't easy, as you might imagine life in the refugee camp—there was no electricity, no water, nothing.

I got lucky. I went to Nairobi through the aid worker. There was a Canadian who worked for a humanitarian organization, who admired me somehow and then she thought that I could go to school because I was very young. And I went to Nairobi.

When I went to Nairobi, I went to school there. I couldn't go back home because there was active civil war and people were being killed there. My family wasn't home. I was hearing news once in a while that they were in Congo; I guess they were in Tanzania.

. . . AMERICA WAS THE FIRST COUNTRY THAT ISSUED ME A VISA TO COME HERE. AND I CAME TO LEARN.

I COULD SEE HOW IN THE FAMILY THAT WE WERE LIMITED BECAUSE OF THE EDUCATION LEVEL WE HAVE. BUT AT THE SAME TIME I CAN SEE THAT IN BURUNDI, THAT WE HAVE KILLED EACH OTHER BECAUSE OF, HONESTLY, ILLITERACY.

I couldn't stay in Nairobi. I ended up going from Nairobi, Kenya to South Africa. I walked. I took [the] bus. I didn't have a passport. It's a long story! But when I reached South Africa, I lived in South Africa for six years.

That's when I started volunteering working with street kids. I ended up going to Geneva working with the World Health Organization and the United Nations High Commission for Refugees, and then I came back to South Africa. I took up another job with an American international organization called the International Rescue Committee for the Ivory Coast.

I started applying for schools. America was the first country that issued me a visa to come here. And I came to learn. Because I am the first in my family that even have finished high school and have finished college.

I could see how in the family that we were limited because of the education level we have. But at the same time I can see that in Burundi, that we have killed each other because of, honestly, illiteracy. In Burundi we have Tutsis and Hutus in tribes, like in Rwanda, and these people, they lived together and one day they were told they were different. And the politicians exploited their ignorance of people, the illiteracy of people. And innocent civilians took up arms; they killed each other. That illiteracy, that ignorance—that's the one I was trying to avoid, and see if I could study, hopefully I would go back to impact my community, my village. I'm glad I came to America. I have really, really learned a lot.

Many people in America failed to be thankful for just the blessing they have. I grew up running miles to go to fetch water. Not even clean water because in my village in Gatumba, there is the Ruzizi River.

There are hippos in that river. There are crocodiles in the river. I remember I used to go to fetch water with other kids. Some of my friends were attacked by crocodiles. And those were dirty water. After we walked mile[s] from that river we will have to go to fetch firewood so that we can prepare [a] meal and we can boil water because we were told to drink water that was boiled.

Now to see in America, people have water. They even wash cars with water, they wash dogs with water. Anything. Sometimes I say, "God, this is injustice. How do kids here, just wait on the door for the school bus to come to take them to school; they go with the bus. I had to walk without shoes, with my pants—the holes—my butt was all outside. And I would go to school hungry, leave the school, go home, and I find there's no meal and I still walk miles.

But the kids who have the school bus, who have food at school, they have computers, they still say they are bored. They say they don't like being alive.

I hear stories from some kids say and I say, "Wow! life can be really sometimes unfair."

I started an exchange program, where I was taking some American students to my village, we build some homes for the poor elderly people.

They had never gone outside of this country. And when they saw other young people like them working hard. In my country, you work hard an entire day just to get paid fifty cents. And you still appreciate life.

The advice I have for people is never give up. There's a time when I felt like the world has fallen on me. There's a time I questioned whether God existed. There's a time I asked, "What have I done to deserve this?" But human beings are resilient people.

As soon as I realized that I could hang on another day, I changed my mindset and attitudes.

I challenged myself not to sit down licking my own wounds. I stood up, and then I said: "No, I deserve better. I don't want to keep feeling sorry for myself-things really changed.

The advice I give to my fellow immigrants who are here in America is to keep the same attitude that we have in Africa. We go to sleep hungry, we work hard. We still hope that today is going to be a better day. We smile, we laugh, we visit each other. We have this proverb called Ubuntu. It means: I exist, because you exist. I am a person because you are a person. We are interconnected. I need you—you need me. That's the spirit that I can ask my fellow human beings who happen to be Americans, to go beyond the individualistic culture, the consumer culture. I didn't have things in my life but I was happy in my village. I didn't even notice we were poor.

If we know each other, if we are brother's keeper or sister's keeper, we will be doing great—we will know how one is doing—how best we can support.

"WE ARE EXPERIENCED ABOUT LIFE"

Immaculee DuSabe and Christophe Nyibizi
Congo

Christophe: My teachers sometimes used to say, "Oh, United States is a very good country. No problems."

Immaculee: I didn't think [the] United States was a cold country. Someone who told me in my country about snow—she told me, "If you touch snow, your finger will be cut off."

And when I heard that, I said, "No one can walk out in the snow." When we came here in November 2012, it was so cold. We didn't have any coats, any shoes, boots. Anything, everything; oh my God! We didn't know anything about this country.

Christophe: [Before] in my country, it was very good.

Immaculee: In my country, there was fighting. War between the people. It was like a conflict between people, which was happening in my country. There was a genocide which happened in Rwanda. After the genocide, the people—killers—came into my country and they start fighting in my county. But [there was] one trouble: they came from Rwanda from Congo to my country.

Life was good for farmer Christophe Nyibizi before tensions between the Hutu and Tutsi became deadly in their country, the Republic of Congo. After their farm was burned down, the family—Christophe's wife, his daughter Immaculee, and her five siblings—fled to safety. Landing eventually in a Rwandan refugee camp, the family of eight endured squalid conditions for eighteen years before getting the opportunity to come to Springfield in 2012. Although they were completely unprepared for the bitterly cold New England winters, they still feel their cup is overflowing.

There were refugees from Rwanda outside of Rwanda. Some were in Burundi. Others were in Uganda. Others were in the Congo.

They left Rwanda and they came to my country and started fighting again because there are Tutsi in Rwanda and Tutsi in my country. So we are Tutsi.

They come from Rwanda and fight in the Congo to kill the Tutsi in the Congo. They start burning houses and everything. Killing cows and people.

Christophe: And they put fire to my house. And we go to a monastery. And we were refugees at the monastery. After six months, again these people

come in to the monastery, again to attack. Red Cross and the UNHCR [United Nations High Commission for Refugees] came in to take the people. They took us to Rwanda.

Immaculee: We didn't have a house. We didn't have calves, we didn't have anything, even education. I grew up in a refugee camp. I don't know my country.

Christophe: Me and my wife we made $40 only a month. I work for $20, my wife make $20. Now I work [for] $8—one hour $8! I make money!!

WHEN WE CAME HERE IN NOVEMBER 2012, IT WAS SO COLD. WE DIDN'T HAVE ANY COATS, ANY SHOES, BOOTS. ANYTHING, EVERYTHING; OH MY GOD! WE DIDN'T KNOW ANYTHING ABOUT THIS COUNTRY.

Immaculee: Our life was so bad. It was good before, and after that we got a problem, which is still happening now. After, we go to refugee camp, and leave refugee camp to come here. We know about good life, bad life, problem[s], poor [poverty], rich—everything. So we are experienced about life.

For me, here is like heaven because I'm good. I go to school, I work, I got money. It's not much, but it's much for me. It's enough because we are free. Everyone is free here. It's not like my country.

I can say that everyone has to thank God because God gives a chance for anyone here in this country. In Africa, the problems are too much.

"ARE YOU OK?"

Hind Mari

Palestine

Even in an educated setting like this one, I have been asked how come my husband allows me to work. Or people assume that by virtue of being Muslim, he must be physically abusive to me—as if that's a given, as if that's everyone's experience. Every single time I open my mouth in a store, or someone hears an accent, immediately: Where are you from? Sometimes they try to ask it like, Oh, do I hear an accent? And that's a code to me for, You don't belong here, where do you belong?

So, with the citizenship, with my involvement in town, with so many things, I am often reminded that, You are an outsider, you are the other. And being a Palestinian means that I don't belong to any of the most-known ethnic groups in this country. When they talk about diversity, diversity means people of African American descent, Asian American, Native American, and Latina/Latino. Nobody would consider Arab American or Palestinian as part of the diversity. I'm often reminded I'm not a person of color enough. According to the [U.S.] State Department, they force me to check the box "white." But I'm not, and I'm not treated as white, and they never will. Early Arab immigrants in the early 1900s, in order to become citizens, had to force the code to accept them as white, because only white people were given citizenship at the time.

Hind Mari came from Palestine to the University of Massachusetts Amherst on a Fulbright scholarship in 1986, expecting to return after completing her master's and doctorate programs. After a tumultuous first visit back to the West Bank, she and her husband, who by then had one child, reluctantly concluded they could not raise a family in their beloved native country. Mari directs the UMass-Amherst's Women of Color Leadership at the Center for Women and Community.

EVERY SINGLE TIME I OPEN
MY MOUTH IN A STORE, OR
SOMEONE HEARS AN ACCENT,
IMMEDIATELY: WHERE ARE
YOU FROM? SOMETIMES THEY
TRY TO ASK IT LIKE, OH, DO
I HEAR AN ACCENT? AND
THAT'S A CODE TO ME FOR,
YOU DON'T BELONG HERE,
WHERE DO YOU BELONG?

Hollywood has done so much damage by only using the stereotypes about us, which means you can never watch a movie that includes a normal Arab or Muslim who happens to be a teacher or a nurse or a judge. You only have to have them be either the rich sheik who is spending money, or the womanizer, or the terrorist. You can never see a normal human being, and I never recognize myself in these.

Even though I'm fifty-three years old, most of my memories are of the Isreali occupation. I was about five and a half years old when the Six-Day War took place in 1967. At that time, my father was working as director of education. It's kind of something like superintendent, but they only had

three for the whole West Bank. And he happened to preside over the largest region of the three. And immediately, the Israeli occupation forces decided that they wanted to ban textbooks from schools. And I think they had a list of about eighty-four books that they wanted to ban, which meant most of the textbooks.

The directors of education decided to go on strike. In early September, when schools were supposed to open after summer vacation, they decided not to. And, my father presiding over the largest one, they came and took him to jail. He was in prison for about six weeks. At the end of six weeks, my uncle was able to secure a visit to go see him, and he took me and my brother who's a year older than me. I remember walking into the room, seeing my father, and getting scared. My father had long hair, a long beard, and I could not recognize him, because every day of his life, my father, literally, shaved. Every single day, he wore suits. To see him in jail, in that scene—I can never forget the room and how he looked and how I felt.

We came in 1986, and unfortunately, within maybe a year and a half, on December 1987, the First Intifada, which is the uprising, started. And I guess that changed things. I still didn't think about staying in the U.S. And my parents, who never wanted to see me living abroad and wanted us to come back, were saying, "Not now . . ."

We went to visit for the first time in six years in 1992, and I think that was the turning point. As Palestinians, we couldn't travel to the airport in Tel Aviv, so we went to Jordan, and from there we went through the bridge to the West Bank. The [Israelis] had two crossing points at the time, one for Palestinians and one for tourists.

We were left to wait almost to the end. It was a Friday. And we asked, "When will our turn come?" We kept being told to wait, and then later a female soldier came to me and asked me to go with her. At the time my son was sleeping on his father's shoulder

and she looked at him and said, "Is that your son?" And I said yes. She said, "Bring him with you, please." So I picked him up sleeping, and we went to a room. She literally strip-searched me completely, in front of my son. He himself woke up being strip-searched. And they took our shoes to be checked by lasers. He started screaming that he wouldn't walk on the filthy floor, and I said, "I will carry you." When we were done, instead of moving us forward, she sent us back to the waiting area again. Ten minutes later, she took our shoes again. By then I'd had it, so I looked at her and I said, "You must be kidding me." I said that in English. She looked at me very blankly and said, "It's the rules." I said, "What could we have done with our shoes? When you have us under surveillance, you've had them ten minutes earlier?" They still took them.

Now, the memory of being strip-searched for my son, the memory of soldiers all over, had completely traumatized him. So it turned out that my son never forgot that memory, even though we tried to talk to a psychiatrist, we tried to deal with it. It came back the first time in fourth grade, when he was asked to write about the best or worst day of your life, and he talked about crossing the borders.

Throughout the visit, it was really, really hard for me to see how everything had become totally different from what I knew. The daily life for people got to be much worse. Later on, my husband and I would refer to our growing up under occupation as the honeymoon of occupation. All the difficulties we had experienced, all the things we had seen growing up under occupation, turned out to be much easier than what people had to deal after the First Intifada. Especially young people and young males could not walk on the streets at night because they could be arrested or harassed for no reason. No one could leave the house without our Israeli IDs—and I would call it the ID that gave me the right to be an occupied inhabitant, not even a citizen.

When I was in college, one of our peers disappeared. He was seen being arrested by the soldiers, and the Israeli authorities claimed they had released him. Nobody had ever seen him being released, and a few days later his body was found dismembered. I remember that guy.

I've been living in this country for twenty-nine years. The first year was in Sunderland, and the last twenty-eight in Amherst. And so of course

THROUGHOUT THE VISIT, IT WAS REALLY, REALLY HARD FOR ME TO SEE HOW EVERYTHING HAD BECOME TOTALLY DIFFERENT FROM WHAT I KNEW. THE DAILY LIFE FOR PEOPLE GOT TO BE MUCH WORSE.

more than half of my life I've been in this town. On a certain level, of course it feels like home. We got married just six weeks before we came to this country, so all my married life has been in this country. At the same time, I feel like a nomad. I know there is an expression called third-culture kid, which is someone who normally grows up in a culture different from their parents'. But I know what I fit is what's called the adult third culture kid, someone who has been away from their country for a very long time, and feels they can never fit in or belong here 100 percent, and can never belong back 100 percent either.

We are incredibly fortunate to have some amazing, amazing friends and a good support system. When I had my daughter, I remember going through the gifts and cards and phone calls congratulating us, and I was overwhelmed with the number of people who had either come to see her or sent postcards or reached out to congratulate us.

A very touching moment was after September 11, 2001. I can't tell you how many phone calls and emails we received asking us, "Are you OK?" I have a friend who is from Minnesota, but she was living in Australia at the time. She literally picked up the phone and said, "We had immediate reactions and hate crimes against Arabs in this area. Are you OK?"

When my son finished high school and we decided to have a graduation party, it was really nice to look around and see how diverse our friends were. So I feel blessed, and Amherst feels like a second home.

"I FEEL LIKE I AM FROM HERE"

Angélica Merino Monge
El Salvador

We left because of the gangs in El Salvador. Also because my mom was a single mother. She couldn't raise three kids on her own. She had two businesses in El Salvador, but it wasn't enough to raise us. So she decided to come here. Her sister let her borrow the money. The day we left, the whole family got together. My grandmother was there, my aunt was there, my cousins, pretty much the close family members were there. And my mom just decided to bring my older brother and I and leave my little brother behind, because at the time he was four years old, so he was too young to travel. I was ten; my brother was eleven. My mom couldn't tell my little brother that we were coming here. She told him that he was going go on vacation with my grandmother for a few days, for a few weeks. And I didn't seem him for nine years after that.

We had an arrangement with a *coyote*, which is a person that brings you here, like a smuggler. And my mom had to pay a lot of money for that. And we knew it was risky, of course; we knew we could die on the way here. We were going to cross the desert—my mom, my brother, and I alone—because once you reach the Mexico and the United States border, the person that brings you just leaves you on the other side. He stays in Mexico, and then you have to figure out your way here from there.

Angelica Merino Monge was ten years old when she, her mother, and her older brother fled El Salvador. She lived here illegally until recently, when the DACA Act (Deferred Action for Childhood Arrivals) was passed, enabling her to become authorized to work and receive deferred action status. Putting herself through college after her mother moved to Maryland for financial reasons, Angelica is committed to encouraging fellow DREAMers (Development, Relief, and Education for Alien Minors [Act]) to be open about their situations. She is one of the organizers of the Out of the Shadows march and president of the Latino International Students' Association at Holyoke Community College.

. . . I STILL FELT ISOLATED FROM EVERYONE ELSE.

We walked for hours. We got here and then we tried to check into a hotel but they told us that we couldn't because we didn't have any papers. So we had to go back and get caught by immigration, and when we were going back it was really dark, it was really cold, and you could hear animals. So of course my brother and I were just crying, my mom didn't know what to do. And then when we're just sitting, there was an immigration truck and they found us. So they took us in and they processed us, and one of the immigration officers told my mom that she was stupid for risking our lives to bring us here. My mom couldn't stop crying. We were separated from her, but we could still hear everything they were telling her. And then they asked us questions like, "Is she really your mom?" "Why are you here?" "Why are you with her?" Those are questions that, when you're ten or eleven, they're shocking. You know, when someone tells you that maybe she's not really your mom. How can they do that to you? And they kept us in a room for a few hours—in a really cold room—and then they let us go.

Back then, they would let you stay for a year, and then you had the choice whether to go to the court or not. And my mom was afraid that if we went to court to plead our case, we'd get deported. So we never went.

I didn't want to go to school. I was depressed; I cried. You know, my mom tried to tell me that it was what my older brother and I were here for. She was here to work, but we were here for an education. And I didn't want to go to school. I mean, kids can be cruel sometimes. Because we didn't speak English, someone would try to talk to me, and I had no idea what they were saying, so they were like, "Oh, you don't talk?" You know, just . . . kids. When I came here in high school, I also struggled. I didn't want to do presentations in my other classes; I didn't want to read out loud because I knew I couldn't. My accent, you know, it's really thick, but it was worse back then. So even though they're more accepting, you still feel that you're not a part of it.

And even though I was more open in this high school, I still felt isolated from everyone else. I couldn't take regular classes like other kids took, and I couldn't take any sports because my mom didn't have any money for that. So I was going to school, going home, and I worked. That was when the problems started, because I knew I wasn't legal. I knew I

I FEEL AMERICAN. I FEEL LIKE
I AM FROM HERE. JUST WITHOUT
THE DOCUMENTS TO PROVE IT.

couldn't work like everyone else. So I kind of started getting angry, because even though I was treated normal as a kid, I wasn't while getting into my adult years. I couldn't do what everyone else could do: I couldn't get a driver's license at sixteen; I couldn't vote; I couldn't get a job—or at least a good job. So that's when my mom explained to us that we were not like everyone else, that we were illegal, and the only way I could work was through getting fake papers. And I got them, and I worked as a dish-washer for a while. I worked about forty-five hours a week, and that's when my mom left.

I thought I had the support to go to college. At least I wouldn't have to pay for rent, so I knew that I was only working towards going to college, towards paying my tuition. But my mom decided to leave because she just couldn't do it anymore. Not here.

At eighteen, you're only a kid. I had to find out how to do everything on my own. And once Obama approved the DACA Act, I went back to school, and I was an in-state tuition student. And I can get a driver's license, but I cannot vote, and I cannot get loans, and that's in only eighteen states. Not all states have approved it—other states, you can only work. So Massachusetts was one of the states that did approve it, which I'm thankful for.

I don't feel like I'm an outsider anymore, but I am. And people just see me as someone else, but they don't know my story. They don't know who I am. They suppose that I am just like them, because I carry conversations like them, and I go to school everyday, and I'm like them . . . but I'm not. So, I think—I feel American. I feel like I am from here. Just without the documents to prove it.

"I WOULD PUT A 'U' IN 'COLOUR'"

Josephine
Ghana

My parents were teachers so, you know, obviously they came for a better life, and also come and see if they can explore, or see if they can get teaching skills, they can apply it here. They just told us one day that they were leaving, so it was kind of a surprise. And I didn't know how it was going to be without them, so it was very hard.

I lived with my aunt, who was very nice, you know, she had six kids and three of us, and also we had house helps, too, that lived with us. So it was a lot of us, we grew up in a big family. And we had some cousins come here and there to visit, too. So we always had a big family all the time.

In the beginning it wasn't normal but, you know, after a while it just becomes normal, because you don't really have a choice. So you still don't have a parent. The communication wasn't like now—you know, if you're well-to-do, you have a telephone, or you know, you have two or three telephones at home. But there wasn't really no cell phones. So, you know, we'd get calls to the house, but it wasn't frequent because it was very expensive for her [Josephine's mom] to call. Because even when I came to America, if you buy a ten-dollar phone card, you would talk for nine minutes. That's like way, years after she came. So you can imagine how much she was paying to just talk to us.

After years of being separated from her parents—both teachers who came to America in search of a better life—Josephine, who wants to be identified only by her first name, finally made it to the United States herself. As luck would have it, a month later her parents returned to Ghana. Josephine was left to fend for herself in a new land. Through hard work, she earned both a bachelor's and master's degree and now has a family. In many ways, she has prospered in this country, but there are certain aspects of American culture she'd rather her children not adopt as their own.

COMING TO AMERICA, I CAME HERE FOR A REASON.

My mom was a citizen, so she filed for all of us to come here to this country. I came here for school, got my bachelor's degree, and also a few years later I went to do my MBA [master of business administration]. Even though I spoke English very well, but I had an accent. People asked, "Oh wow, you have an accent, where you from?" You know, it's like, you go to school, the professor is speaking, and they speak so quick. And you're trying to make notes, but before you make it, before you hear the word and make the notes, it's just too late, cause they are already gone to the next, you know. So it was very tough for me. I had to stay up extra hours to study. And finally I decided to tape my courses, because if I tape it, then I have to go home and listen to it so many times in order to really understand what they were trying to say, so that I can get it, because it wasn't easy.

Ghana is like an English system in England. And I remember one teacher told me, "If you write that English language here in America, I am going

to fail you." I remember that. Because I was writing good essays, but the spellings—like, you know, "labour," I would put "u" in it, and "colour," I would put "u" in it—and she was really penalizing me for that. And it wasn't encouraging at all, because she was always giving me, "You can't make it in this country."

With school, too, I saw some kind of racism a little bit too, but I didn't care, because I was ready to move on and get a better life. And my education was my goal. So when you live in Ghana or Africa, everything is totally opposite. You know, if you're born and bred in a different country and you're used to everything there, you know, we're not used to the snow and the cold, and the this and the that.

One thing I miss is that—in America, even when you're sleeping, you're thinking about how many hours you're sleeping, because you have to go, or you have something to do. But over there, for some reason, your mind is relaxed. You do stuff, you get stuff going, but your mind is very relaxed. And there's a lot of family members around you, and kids can go to their neighbors' and play, and when your kids are not home, you're not worried, "Oh my God, what happened," because you don't have to worry about too much guns, and too much this and that. When I came here, I don't see a lot of people outside. But in Ghana, you see like after kids come back from school, you see them playing outside—they finish their homework, they are out playing. They are running, they doing this and that. Every time I see Halloween, how kids go around, that's how Ghana is.

Coming to America, I came here for a reason. Don't lose your culture and your mannerism. Because with us, respect is everything. So you don't lose it. Because I can't tell you how many people meet me and be like, "Oh my God, you respect so much," and, you know, "You are well-mannered." And it's good because some people can change their behavior just because they been around you for a long time. So I think that's a very good thing that people should not lose.

ONE THING I MISS IS THAT— IN AMERICA, EVEN WHEN YOU'RE SLEEPING, YOU'RE THINKING ABOUT HOW MANY HOURS YOU'RE SLEEPING, BECAUSE YOU HAVE TO GO, OR YOU HAVE SOMETHING TO DO. BUT OVER THERE, FOR SOME REASON, YOUR MIND IS RELAXED.

"I WAS BLACKLISTED"

Magda Ahmed

Sudan

I left Sudan like six months into the coup d'etat, which they were just start-ing against different people. And I went out to work. I was working with an American organization already, then I took a job with them in Yemen to leave Sudan and be closer, but we have double names, like your paper has a name, and the name you use in-country is a different one. So sometimes, if you're lucky, you can go out. My husband was not so lucky. He was jailed and then after that, we had to sneak him out with a different name and a different way. It took about two years of planning to get him out.

I could not go back to Sudan because I was blacklisted. I have to stay in Yemen without even packing.

I wanted to come to America from Yemen because of the civil war in Yemen. I left Yemen on a contract for four years and my contract was expiring and there was no way to go back to Sudan. So I just applied. We came on a student visa. And then we applied for political asylum. And we have to sit down and revisit why we left Sudan, how we went to Yemen, and how we came from Yemen to here. And that was not an easy trip to revisit, especially for my husband. He was tortured, he was still traumatized with that. It took a lot of work to get the story out.

Magda Ahmed was born, raised, and educated in Sudan. Blacklisted in 1989 shortly after the coup d'etat organized by the Muslim Brotherhood, she fled to Yemen with her two young daughters. Her husband, a political prisoner at the time, managed to follow two years later. When civil war broke out in Yemen, the family came to the United States on student visas. Eventually they sought and were granted political asylum. She lives in Amherst and works for the United States Agency for International Development.

When we left Yemen to come to America, we came only with our passport. We left everything because of the war. I left my car, my home, my money—everything. We just had ourselves and we left. We were evacuated with the military plane from Sana'a, in Yemen, to Saudi Arabia. And we got the American consulate and the Sudanese consulate—they both came to the airport. And then we got our visas to come straight here to Boston.

When I drove here in Boston, it was crazy. But I drove in Yemen. I thought, "You know what? If I can drive in Yemen, I [can] drive anywhere." But I found Bostonians to be worse than the Yemeni in driving.

We could not develop a taste in the beginning. The pizza—that stuff was not tasty. Even the salad did not taste the same. The tomatoes, the cucumber. Even something simple as peanut butter. It has sugar in it. It took me a year or two to discover that you can get the natural one that doesn't have any sugar added. We eat the peanut butter as a sauce, actually with chili. It's a hot sauce, you dip meat in it and you eat it that way. You make it as a salad. So when the sugar were there, the first time I did it I have to dump it all. It was just too sugarized for us to go ahead and eat that.

For grocery shopping, it was a nightmare. You go for the cheese, there are like ten, twenty, twelve different kinds of cheeses. We have only like one or two. You don't like white cheese? It is white cheese. You don't have that much option. But the options here are like uncountable. You go for shopping, I get headaches. I stopped doing shopping. My husband is the one doing the shopping. And then you need to read the labels, I can't do that.

I don't feel like an American yet. And when I go home, I feel like I'm missing home here, too. I still feel like I have to differentiate when I said "home" and then I have to say "home in Sudan" or "home in America."

I think my mistake and my husband's too and that's maybe why I still don't feel 100 percent Americanized, is that we were always going back home. That was the plan. We were here going to school; after school, we are going home. This government will change; we are going home. I was crying my eyes out when I have to . . . like . . . go do my citizenship exam because I did not want to leave my nationality. And then I was happy when I know that I can keep both of them; that's what made it easy for me to decide. But getting involved in the community you live in—I volunteered into the Amherst Commission, I volunteered with the graduate students, I started working, I bought a home. We started, you know, feeling that this is home.

I STILL FEEL LIKE I HAVE TO DIFFERENTIATE WHEN I SAID "HOME" AND THEN I HAVE TO SAY "HOME IN SUDAN" OR "HOME IN AMERICA."

I WAS CRYING MY EYES OUT
WHEN I HAVE TO . . . GO
DO MY CITIZENSHIP EXAM
BECAUSE I DID NOT WANT TO
LEAVE MY NATIONALITY.

"A MOMENT OF VALIDATION"

Rogelio Miñana
Spain

I'm from beautiful Valencia, which is the east coast of Spain, where the weather is nice and the winters are very mild. I left Spain in a time of a deep economic crisis and high unemployment, and so I came to the U.S. because I wanted to do a Ph.D. in Spanish and be a college professor. And so I went to Canada first when I was twenty-two years old, I went to Canada for my master's, and then I came to the States for my Ph.D. In that sense, I came in a certain privilege, because I had a student visa, I had papers, I had an education, I spoke some English—not a lot, but some—and I came into an environment which really embraced me and nurtured me and allowed me to become the college professor that I am today. So I'm very grateful to Ottawa University in Canada for my master's and Penn State University here in the States for the support that they gave me.

I think it's pretty common for all of us when we leave our countries as students to think that we're eventually gonna go back to our countries, our home countries. We come here, get an education, and usually we think at the time—at least that's what happened to all my cohort of fellow students, graduate students—that we all thought we would go back eventually to our country. I think that maybe 95 percent of us stayed in the states. So what happens is first of all that it's hard to go back because at some point

Former Mount Holyoke College professor Rogelio Miñana hails from Valencia, Spain. Coming to the United States in his twenties for graduate study in Spanish, he fully intended to return to his native country. But as professional opportunities began opening up for him here, Miñana decided to make the United States his permanent home. Having lived in a number of U.S. cities and traveled a good deal for his work, he regards himself to be a global citizen whose life is decidedly richer for having called so many places home. But the real sign to him of his acceptance as an American in the eyes of his peers was when he was offered the position of chair of Mount Holyoke's Spanish Department.

I ALWAYS THINK OF MY EXPERIENCE AS AN IMMIGRANT AS A PROCESS OF ENRICHMENT AND ADDITION, AS OPPOSED TO SIMPLY YOUR TRADITIONAL NOTION OF ASSIMILATION. BECAUSE TO ME, ASSIMILATION SOUNDS MORE LIKE YOU GOTTA LOSE PART OF WHO YOU ARE TO BECOME SOMETHING THAT YOU'RE NOT.

you—you're not part of that society anymore. You have been educated here, you grow up professionally in this country, and going back to your home country would be probably harder than staying here. At the same time, you never feel quite at home here, because you grew up somewhere else, and your—most of my family, in my case, are still in Spain.

There were two critical steps towards feeling more at home here. One was the first time that my parents visited with me. I had been here for about three years at the time, and when they came, they didn't speak English, any English, and for the first time I was kind of like my parents' parent. And that really changed our relationship completely. When I went back to Spain a few months later and I stayed with them, they really treated me differently. They thought of me as someone who had grown up, I guess, and who had been able to adapt to another country and be functional in another country and speak the language and, you know, get a Ph.D., etc. So that was really a very special moment for me.

The other moment was when I got hired at Mount Holyoke College as chair of the Spanish department, because that was a professional validation that I wasn't expecting. When I first applied for jobs, I'm a Spanish teacher, Spanish professor, and so part of my job interviews were conducted in Spanish. So in the end I always felt that I was going back to my native language and my native culture. But when I interviewed for this position as chair of the Spanish Department, the whole thing was in English, it all happened in English. Because when you apply for a senior position, then things go through the senior administration and all the interview process and everything is in English. And getting the offer and accepting the job that I had interviewed for in English—you know, I had to lay out a vision for the department, I had to demonstrate that I was capable of handling

I THINK IT'S PRETTY COMMON FOR ALL OF US WHEN WE LEAVE OUR COUNTRIES AS STUDENTS TO THINK THAT WE'RE EVENTUALLY GONNA GO BACK TO OUR COUNTRIES, OUR HOME COUNTRIES.

a department from an administrative point of view—not just my teaching, my research, but also just dealing with the whole academic infrastructure. That, for me, that was a beautiful moment. That was a moment of validation and a moment of affirmation.

And a few years later I became a U.S. citizen. But for me, I had really sort of made it, right, I had at some point felt like I was really part of this society, especially when I got that first job.

I always think of my experience as an immigrant as a process of enrichment and addition, as opposed to simply your traditional notion of assimilation. Because to me, assimilation sounds more like you gotta lose part of who you are to become something that you're not.

A lot of who I am, I try to treasure that, and share it with others. I like to eat, and I like to take my time to eat. And that's something that's very important to me, and I want to make sure that my friends and the people who surround me and sometimes even my students know that. That sort of joy of life that my culture has given me, I think that's something that a lot of people in the U.S. have told me that they appreciate.

"I WON THE LOTTERY"

Nayomi Dasanayake
Sri Lanka

After I married, my husband tried to go to Italy because he didn't make more money. He was a government servant, but the Sri Lankan government didn't pay a lot, so he tried to go to Italy to make money. However, during that time I applied for the green card lottery. The U.S. government every year does a lottery that we can apply to online. So the very first time, I won the lottery! So we decided to come here.

When I talked with some people, they told me that they applied six times, seven times, but they didn't get it. However, the very first time, I got it. I was very happy and I was excited, but at the same time also I felt so sad, because I had to leave my parents, siblings, and my small country, so I didn't want to come. But the economic problems made us come here. My father, he was not happy; but my mom, she was very happy. Because she thought that if I go here, I can settle down, I can succeed in life. So she was very happy, and my siblings were also very happy.

Within six months, we left our country. I felt so sad, because I left my siblings, country, my parents. And at that time also we had problems, because we need money for the visa, but we didn't have that much money. I asked my brother. He gave money for the visa; and for the ticket, my mom gave me the money. In Sri Lankan rupees, two lakhs for a visa, it means

Nayomi Dasanayake and her husband wanted to improve their circumstances, so were planning to leave Sri Lanka to live in Italy. But before that plan materialized, she won the Green Card lottery, and the couple emigrated to New England instead. Dasanayake feels her new life in America really began the moment she began taking English classes.

67

$2,000. After we won the lottery, they asked us to find a person who can sponsor us because after we come here one person has to help us to find a place to live and to find a job. One of my father's friends lives in Westfield, Massachusetts. He gave us a letter that he can help us. Straightly we came to Westfield.

First he helped us to find a job for my husband, and after that we lived with them three months. After that, we moved to a different place. First he [husband] found a job in a gas station, and he had to make pizza in the gas

station, because it's pizza and gas, both. After that, he found another job, also in a gas station. That job also didn't work for him, because that manager didn't give more hours to work. So we had to move to Connecticut. He didn't show anything, but I know he felt bad, because he's very educated. At that time we didn't have a car or a bicycle or anything. I remember that he walked twenty minutes to go to work, sometimes in bad weather, in the snow. He told me that he fell down on the snow and he hurt his leg. After one year, he told me all the things. Until that, he didn't tell me anything: he said he's okay, "I can do it, I'm your daughter's' father, so don't worry, we can do it." That's it.

I started my new life in Hartford, Connecticut. Because one of my friends told me that there are ESL classes at the Hartford Public Library, so straight I went to the Hartford Public Library and I asked, "I want to take classes at the library." So they got my telephone number and the name, and they told me that they are going to call me. Next day, they called me; that Wednesday I went to the library, and I think I put my first step to achieve my goals.

I am a mom, but I'm taking classes at Capital Community College. And my daughter, she goes to a good school. She's able to have a good education here. My husband is also taking classes at Jubilee House. He tries to improve his English skills. And I also make some money. My husband makes a little more money. And we have fun places to enjoy. Because in Sri Lanka we don't have a lot of fun places, especially for kids. Because if we go somewhere, they're supposed to go with us. But sometimes it's not really fun for them. But here, they have a lot of fun places: they have a lot of opportunities like summer camp, science centers, museums. Sometimes they are free. So I think we have a lot of opportunities to succeed in our life.

. . . THAT WEDNESDAY I WENT TO THE LIBRARY, AND I THINK I PUT
MY FIRST STEP TO ACHIEVE MY GOALS.

"I ALMOST LOST MY LIFE"

Woodlyn Joachim
Haiti

I almost lost my life before I even had the chance to have it. I don't know if that makes sense. But when my mom got pregnant with me, her own family members, they wanted to end her pregnancy, because they said, "Well, you're Christian. You're not married. You're having a kid." Every single woman in my family—every single one of them—they actually did the same thing: they got pregnant before they got married. So the men came up with the idea that the women are actually the ones who are cursing the family and keeping us in poverty, because they're getting kids without getting married, and that's a curse. So what they did is, they abused my mother emotionally and physically, so that they could end the pregnancy. However, thanks to God, my mom had a healthy baby. So she decided that she's going to protect me, and she's going to make everything that she can to offer me a brighter future—offer me an education—because she knew that [pregnancy outside of marriage] wasn't the reason for us being poor. It was the lack of education in the family. So that's why education has always been a big part of my life.

For immigrants, when you hear the United States, you hear the country of light, the newest technology, hope, education. Those were all the words that made me really happy and blessed, made me feel really blessed for coming

University of Connecticut student Woodlyn Joachim and her mother had been waiting for visas to leave Haiti long before the massive earthquake struck in 2011, leaving them homeless. But the wish of Woodlyn's mother to raise her daughter in a country with more options for women was granted shortly thereafter. Joachim credits her decision to pursue her dream to become a pediatric oncologist to the encouragement she received from staff of the Boys and Girls Club of Hartford, where she was awarded youth of the year in 2014.

here. However, when I came here, I was blessed. I mean, I went from going to school on foot—walking two miles, even more, every day back and forth to go to school—to having free buses to actually take me there. From not having electricity for a week, or even a year, to having electricity 24/7. From not having clean water to having clean water, actual clean water. Stuff that people actually take for granted. And one thing I saw that is that teachers here, they're like your second parent. They care about you. But in Haiti, they don't really. All they care about is making the money, and that's it. But here, if they see you crying, they come to you and say, "Hey, are you okay? Is everything okay? How can I help? I want to help. How can I help? Please." They actually ask you to have your permission for them to help you. And that was really amazing to see all those people surrounding you, and they want to hug you and they want to support you. But then there are students who just don't see that as a blessing. That's why, unless you don't have something, you don't really see the importance of it. And I imagined that kids would be more respectful towards the teachers, but I actually saw the opposite. Not for all students, but there were many students who really took that for granted.

My uncle gave me a French-English dictionary, so in the cafeteria I would be sitting and reading the dictionary. And students would come up to me and say, "Are you reading a dictionary?" I'd say, "Yeah, it's a book, right? What's wrong with reading a dictionary? I'm just learning." And they're like, "Oh, okay. . . . weird."

I love it here because of the freedom. I mean, as cheesy as this may sound, I feel like in America we do have problems, such as gender inequality, racial inequality, and whatsoever, but comparing to other places, it's better. And it can get better. And I feel like we're that nation where we're always willing to help others. Like if there's war in a place, we are always willing to go there and help. If there's something going on, America is that country where you can feel welcomed, and it's different.

I'm both an American me and a Haitian me. When I came here, I was introduced to feminism, and that's actually why I decided to apply to minor in women's and gender studies. When I told my cousin in Haiti—well, he's my cousin, but I call him Uncle because he's kind of older—I told him, "I want to become a doctor" when I was really young, and he laughed at me.

And I said, "Why are you laughing?" He said, "Oh, you're a woman, you're a girl, so you need to stay home, cook for your husband and your kids." "Why do you feel like a guy can be a doctor, but I can't? You can't make my future." So I feel like I'm an American me in terms of believing in equal rights in every aspect of everyone's life. No matter who you are and no matter what you identify yourself as, you should have the same rights as everyone else.

I remember I was in my bedroom. I'd just bought this cute little cat, and he was about three months old, and we were watching TV together. And my mother was in the kitchen and she was cooking her favorite food. It's very famous, because it's soupe joumou, which is a soup that we cook every year

I ALMOST LOST MY LIFE BEFORE I EVEN HAD THE CHANCE TO HAVE IT.

to celebrate New Year's Eve. And so we were cooking—she was cooking, and I was watching TV—and then I kind of heard a sound that I never heard before. And then after that the earth started to shake. And then my mother ran to me and she said, "It's an earthquake! Let's run!" So we ran together and we stood under the door, the entrance of the house. And then the walls were shaking. I remember my mother taking her hand and kind of stopping a wall from falling on my head where we were standing, and we were screaming, like "Jesus, Jesus." We didn't know what was happening, we could see neighbors running everywhere.

And one very clear image that I have is of my best friend, who I actually lost during the earthquake. Because she was running down the stairs, and then a wall fell on her. And that happened in front of me. And the sad thing is that this wall that protected my home—at least the place that I used to call home—that wall where when we were little we would draw stuff on, and say "best friends forever." And just to see her under there, it was really emotional. I couldn't really cry when it happened. It really affected me afterwards, because I had nightmares. I really could not stop thinking about it. I couldn't really focus in school. And so it was really difficult, and it was a scary experience.

I had to live in a tent with just my mom. And as you know, living in a very poor country like that, just two women in a small tent, living among hundreds of people, where people were getting sick, they were dying. Young girls just like me, the same age as me, were getting raped. It was very scary. We had no one to protect us except for our prayers. So we were dependent on God. That was our only hope.

And I remember during those nine months, my actual only hope for a brighter future was actually going to school. Because knowing that my high school was the only place that I could go to where the buildings were still standing, there were still walls to protect me, there were people around me that gave me hope—that told me that, okay, there's still hope for a brighter future. So I went to school every single day, just knowing the fact that there is actually a place where I can go and learn, and prepare myself for the real world.

I'M BOTH AN AMERICAN ME
AND A HAITIAN ME.

INITIALLY I CAME ONLY FOR SIX MONTHS.

"WOMEN AROUND THE WORLD"

Manju Sharma
India

Initially I came only for six months. And my husband was postdoctoral research fellow with Michigan State University at the moment, so I came as a spouse of a postdoc. Leaving India was hard, but at the same time, it was just like, I am going to travel, not to stay. And once we were here it changes, and you change your mind.

My husband decided to apply for green card, and when I asked that, you know, "You are done with your education, we are heading back?" and he said, "No, it helps to have some kind of training after doing your Ph.D., and this is my second chance of getting a training. At the same time, I have to get some visa status which let me stay for it."

I liked it right away, being here also, but as a postdoctoral research fellow's wife, I had very little opportunity for social connections, and that was hard at the moment. So the first year was very hard and I really wanted to go back, but my husband was looking for a job so we moved to Fort Collins, Colorado, and that came out much better because it was [a] new place for both of us. And I volunteered in church groups and Women Around the World, and that opened up a whole new world for me. It really helped me, not like I'm helping them, but it helped me more, I think. And it energized me to do more in the community, and that's how I was, having a connection

Manju Sharma was happily living in the state of Himemachalpradesh in northern India in 1987 when her husband was accepted to do postdoctoral research here. She left India for what she believed would be a half year of travel, and looked forward to returning to her job teaching chemistry at a local college. But her husband found work in the United States once his studies ended. Staying busy by helping others was what saw her through the first years here, which were lonely for her at times. Now, nearly thirty years later, in addition to working as a chemistry technician at UMass-Amherst, Manju serves on the Board of Directors at the Survival Center in Amherst and as the Hindu advisor to students at both Mount Holyoke College and Amherst College.

in the community was most important for me. And I feel equally at home in both place[s] now, I'm fortunate enough to do that, but not many people do that.

Both cultures have so many wonderful things to offer; at the same time, if you could eliminate some, both ways, and that would be a great society. But it's not that easy, it's easier said than done, because people are people, they grow up with certain values and certain way of living, and that's how the social evils or social status are developed. And I admire the great things both have and I really admire the structure part over here, the social structure. And people keep the data handy for everybody, they share the infor-

mation so easily. Back home, most of the things, even the home remedies and everything, nobody wanted to write it down. It's just passed on, as a story. And I think a lot of information gets lost. India has a lot of problem[s] with the caste system, or the weddings, the way weddings are done with a lot of expenditure and people even have to borrow money.

I really love the weddings over here. People decide they want to do it the Saturday afternoon, two hours, and that's how much they want to spend, and it's wonderful because people do not undergo debt for it. Not every common person follows that route. And over there, because everybody thinks they have to do an extraordinary affair for the wedding and they

have to go out of their way to borrow money, and the couple is starting a new life, and they're starting with a lot of debt for appearances, going under debt for that. And this is something we cannot help, but I think, seeing both sides, I love the way people do [it] over here. If you want to go under debt, that's fine, but you don't have to, that's great.

... SO WE MOVED TO FORT COLLINS, COLORADO, AND THAT CAME OUT MUCH BETTER BECAUSE IT WAS [A] NEW PLACE FOR BOTH OF US. AND I VOLUNTEERED IN CHURCH GROUPS AND "WOMEN AROUND THE WORLD," AND THAT OPENED UP A WHOLE NEW WORLD FOR ME.

"IT TOOK A VERY LONG TIME"

Heap Sin
Cambodia

I consider myself a Cambodian American, because the majority of my life is in the United States. I was only raised in Cambodia for eleven years, and none of those years were happy. There were wars, fighting all the time, atrocity—that's all we saw. But we came here. We have memories, but we are able to suppress those atrocities and continue with our lives.

Most people who left their country have different reasons. But we basically didn't have an option. We either leave, or we possibly die, from either starvation or killing. So my parents decided to leave the country so that we as children have a chance at surviving atrocity. After the Khmer Rouge, my parents decided Cambodia is not a place to raise us. They heard that there were refugee camps around the borders, and there was UN [United Nations] aid and people and countries taking those refugees to overseas, like France, the United States, and Japan.

The new government was really strict also—they didn't want any people leaving the country. We walked at night and we stayed in the bush during the day. It took us three nights to arrive at the borders. That's where the UN provides food and shelter. We lived there for about two or three years. And then there was intensive fighting going on. We packed our stuff at six o'clock every day, just ready for if the fighting would start. And one day

As an adolescent, Heap Sin and his family escaped Cambodian communist forces on foot. After ten years in a squalid Thai refugee camp, the family obtained visas to come to Massachusetts. Knowing little English when he arrived in his early twenties, Heap attended public high school in Amherst, Massachusetts, graduating—he likes to say he's his school's oldest graduate ever—at the age of twenty-four. A couple of degrees later, Heap now works as a human resource information specialist at Amherst College.

my father decided that we were going to sneak into the refugee camps in Thailand. It's called Khao-I-Dang.

The government, but also the bandit and the freedom fighters, if they caught us, we could be punished severely. They would send all the children to our village, and my parents would be sent to the borders, to work in the concentration camps, to build the fence around the border. That's one fear; the other fear was the bandits. If we have gold or any money, any valuable belonging, they probably won't kill us; but if you don't have anything, they'd most likely kill us. And the other fear is the freedom fighter. They might suspect us of spying or something, and they also could torture us and kill us.

We sneaked into Thailand, into the camp. Most people who were in that camp were transported by the UN from the borders. But they closed that transport: they said they don't want anymore refugees into the camp. So my father said, "Well, why don't we just sneak in?" It took us about half a night. We left the border around five or six o'clock in the evening, and we arrived at the camp probably around four, five o'clock. But we kept hiding, because the guard was frequently walking around. So when there were gaps within the shift, my father saw the opportunity, so we sneaked in. After we ran in halfway, they saw us, they shot at us.

A couple of rounds. And fortunately, we just ran into the population and disappeared.

When we arrived here in 1988, we were so shocked. Totally lost. We didn't know where to go places, even markets, supermarkets to buy food, to find jobs, or anything. But our sponsors, they were really helpful.

It took a very long time, I would say four years, before I felt really comfortable to go anywhere, to really say, I can survive in this country. Fortunately, we have a system that could help our new arrival at that time. My first and second years, I was very lost. Everything so new—the language, the system. You know, we were farmers.

I never went to school in Cambodia, so learning a new language is such a big task. Not to mention finding a job.

But, because we have a system, I hope that we continue to invest in our new immigrants, because I am the proof of the Massachusetts and Amherst school system's investment in education, in immigrants. In my life, I would

MOST PEOPLE WHO LEFT THEIR COUNTRY HAVE DIFFERENT REASONS. BUT WE BASICALLY DIDN'T HAVE AN OPTION. WE EITHER LEAVE, OR WE POSSIBLY DIE, FROM EITHER STARVATION OR KILLING.

never imagine that I'd have the opportunity to go to school—not to mention the university—but I had that opportunity. I'm very grateful that my sponsor brought me to enroll in school. When they asked us what we wanted to do, I said, "Well, if I could, we want to go to school." So they enrolled us.

I was twenty-three, twenty-four, maybe, when I graduated from high school. And then, fortunately, I have a woman who worked at the Asian Center at UMass. One day I got out of high school, and I was in my senior year, and she asked me, "What do you want to do after high school?" I said, "Well, find a job." And she was like, "Don't you want to go to college or advanced education?" I said, "Yeah, but I don't have money." But she said, "Well, let me help you." And I said, "Well, thank you." And she guided me through financial aid, all the applications and things, and finally I got accepted to UMass. For normal people they graduate in four years, but I was so smart it took me six years to graduate.

I'm very grateful to be here. I want us to, as an American—I consider myself an American—to invest in our new immigrants. We are the land of immigrants, and we have to accept our new immigrants, just like the generation before us accepted us. And we have to accept our new generation of immigrants also.

IT TOOK A VERY LONG TIME, I WOULD SAY FOUR YEARS, BEFORE I FELT REALLY COMFORTABLE TO GO ANYWHERE, TO REALLY SAY, I CAN SURVIVE IN THIS COUNTRY.

WHEN I WAS GROWING UP, TAIWAN WAS UNDER JAPANESE OCCUPATION. SO I WAS BORN JAPANESE. MY FIRST LANGUAGE WAS JAPANESE. AND AFTER THE SECOND WORLD WAR, TAIWAN WAS RETURNED TO CHINA. THEN I BECAME CHINESE.

"TO BE TOLERANT PEOPLE"

Ching Ching Cernada

Taiwan

I've been in this country for fifty years and the change of my attitude toward a lot of things, especially, like, marriage. When I came, our parents or ourselves always felt you should marry people from your own country. But I think most of our children are married to Americans or people from other countries. And it seems like the line between country, race, and the nationality has become very mixed now. For instance, my daughter sometimes would say, "She's half Chinese, half American." But by the time . . . her children's generation, I think they won't be claiming they have Chinese heritage.

When I was growing up, Taiwan was under Japanese occupation. So I was born Japanese. My first language was Japanese. And after the Second World War, Taiwan was returned to China. Then I became Chinese. There wasn't any private car. The main transportation was rickshaw.

It was very difficult to get out of Taiwan. The only people can get out is students come here for graduate study. Just like everybody else! I thought that was the automatic future for graduates. At that time, Taiwan was under martial law; there was no freedom. I wasn't that anxious to leave. It was more of my parents' wish.

Ching Ching Cernada is a retired health educator raised in Taipei, Taiwan. After a year of graduate work in the United States, she married an American and returned with him to her native country. Ten years later, she and her family decided they preferred life in America, settling eventually in the Amherst area.

Everybody thought, we would be coming to a place like the New York City. My port of entry was Seattle. Then I flew to Chicago to stay with my cousin for a few days. And Chicago is a big city. I came from Taipei, that is a very big city. So Chicago, I thought, "Well, this is America." But I took the Greyhound [bus] from Chicago to Bloomington. Along the way, it was so deserted and lonely looking. I started to cry on the bus.

Sometimes you see one house and for thirty minutes there's nothing. And I wondered, "Where are the neighbors? How do they get in touch with friends?"

When I arrived, that was still in the summertime. When I first saw the dandelion, I thought, "Wow, what a beautiful field!" Then next day, I saw them mowing down the dandelions, and I thought, "Oh, what a waste!"

I remember I had quite a lot of language difficulty. We study English in middle school and high school. So I had six, seven years of English. But what I learned in textbooks is sometime not prepare myself for the daily conversation. I remember the first instant I felt so puzzled was I bought something at the Greyhound station and then the guy said, "A buck and half." I learned one cent is also called a penny, or five cents is called nickel, but I never learned "buck!" So I was puzzled. What is a buck? And half of what?

SOME OF THE AMERICANS, A FEW OF THEM, HAVE PREJUDICE AGAINST PEOPLE FROM OTHER COUNTRIES. IF THEY CANNOT UNDERSTAND THE FOREIGNER'S LANGUAGE, THEY FELT, "WHO CAN UNDERSTAND YOU?" THAT KIND OF ATTITUDE, RATHER THAN THINKING, "WOW, OTHER PEOPLE ARE BILINGUAL!" A LOT OF AMERICANS ONLY SPEAK ENGLISH.

At this time, point in my life, of course, my husband is here, my children and grandchildren are all here. And also, I have lived in U.S. much longer than in Taiwan. And also my parents are gone and my family home is not there anymore. So, I don't feel Taiwan is my home anymore. But while my parent[s] were still alive, I felt Taiwan is still home.

Some of the Americans, a few of them, have prejudice against people from other countries. If they cannot understand the foreigner's language, they felt, "Who can understand you?" that kind of attitude, rather than thinking, "Wow, other people are bilingual!" A lot of Americans only speak English.

I'd like to make Americans realize it's good to take up a second language or third language. Also, be tolerant of people who speak with an accent or use wrong expression.

I CAME AS A REFUGEE. LIKE OTHER
REFUGEES WHEN YOU COME, THEY ASK
YOU TO FORGET YOUR BACKGROUND.
YOU START EVERYTHING LIKE FRESH.

"DON'T FORGET WHO YOU ARE"

Georges Annan-Kingsley
Cote D'Ivoire

I was working at a university, I was having a good salary. I was having my own business, an interior decoration company, and I was also engaged in politics in my country. And because of political problems that happened in my country after an election, there was a mess. Through the UN [United Nations], the French government there was a civil war in my country. And I had to hide myself for two months. And when I came out I was feeling weak, tired, and everything, and when I was able to go see a doctor they found out, I was having a kidney failure.

I couldn't stay in my country because there was people were in house arrests, people were targets, so I couldn't stay. My workshop was burned. I couldn't stay. My salary was frozen, so I needed to go out of the country to continue doing my dialysis. So I have to go to the next country, which was Ghana, and it is my country where I was born. And there I had the opportunity in the past of working with the French Embassy as a diplomat for them. So I had some connections to people that I know there. So I went back to Ghana to stay there. And I spent two years in Ghana.

And it was not easy because many of the [political] prisoners went there, but they could not have status of refugees because of some other considerations. It was hard because most of them had to leave their families and

Georges Annan-Kingsley was a successful artist and university-level art teacher in Cote d'Ivoire, when, he was forced to flee to Ghana because of political unrest. For two years, the Ghanaian government sheltered him, but when funds for dialysis ran out, the Ghanaian Catholic clergy helped Annan-Kingsley, his wife, and son come to the United States on a medical visa. In Hartford, as he hopes and waits for a kidney transplant, Georges continues to paint and teach.

everything, and I left my family also. I left my wife and child, I left them because I didn't want them to go with me. I didn't know what I am going to face. So I preferred for them to stay in Cote d'Ivoire, be with their family, safe somewhere, and me going to the adventure.

I was in Ghana, and in Ghana they denied me medical care with my kidney failure because they say I have to pay. And the amount involved was so much. Each dialysis that you have to do there was around three hundred dollars that you have to pay cash—where am I going to make that money? And you have to pay for three months in advance. So it was not possible; I was just having about one hundred dollars in my pocket! So it was a little bit hard. I stayed more than three months without doing my dialysis.

By the help of God, I was able to meet a former ambassador that know
me and that knowed what I've done for the Ghanaian government. When
they did their fifty years anniversary, I did all the history of fifty years of
Ghana government in seventeen art paintings. And I give it to them as the
anniversary gift. I was in Cote d'Ivoire when I did it to them. And when it
was received in that time—it was in 2007—I was received at that time by
the Ghanaian president at his office in Ghana, and he wanted to give me a
check for that and I refused. I said "I know that I'm an Ivorian, but I know
also that a part of my blood is coming from Ghana. And I can't deny it. So
it's my way of saying thank you to the government of Ghana, the Republic of
Ghana. So I don't want any money."

BUT IN AFRICA, I WAS TEACHING ARTISTS! I WAS MAKING THEM BE ARTISTS. AND SOME OF THEM ARE RUNNING IN THE WORLD AND HAVING EXHIBITIONS AND EVERYTHING. AND WHEN YOU COME HERE AND THEY WILL TELL YOU, "NO. WE DON'T KNOW, BECAUSE YOU DIDN'T GO TO SCHOOL IN AMERICA."

So I refused the money that the government wanted to give me.

The government decide to reward me through UNESCO [United Nations Education, Science and Cultural Organization], and they did the documents. But the next government who came did not follow up, and they (the documents) were somewhere there.

When I came back in 2011, five years after I'd been sick, I met that ambassador and he remembered that they did something. So he was able to go back to the document and see what they did, and from there he sent my document to the French Embassy to see how best they can help. And also another document to the new government. So I went to the French government embassy, and they pushed UNESCO, whose headquarters are in Paris. So they pushed UNESCO in Paris, and UNESCO say, yes, my name is on the list of the people who have to be rewarded in West Africa for what they have done in art.

But really the UNESCO then did not follow up. So the embassy tried to push the people in Ghana; they did something on the TV on what I did. And the minister of culture in Ghana took my document to see UNHCR [United Nations High Commissioner for Refugees] so the French Embassy, the UNHCR, the UN and UNESCO, and the Ghanaian government altogether did a meeting and decided to take me in charge; for two years they were paying for my dialysis. For two years!

In Ghana after three months without dialysis I was in the way of dying, when one day I had a call and they told me, "We are now taking you in charge."

I came as a refugee. Like other refugees when you come, they ask you to forget your background. You start everything like fresh. So when I came, I had to forget that I was teaching at a university. Who's going to employ me? And I have a health issue.

At the same time, I was saying that I'm an intellectual; you can't shut the mouth of an intellectual or the brain of an intellectual. It's not possible. So I make a strategy of how to come out. I start—the first thing I say I have to make a collection of painting and sculpture to do my exhibition. And I was able to do in six months, I was able to do an exhibition.

It happened because I know that I have to support my family. So the first thing I did: after a week, I went around seeing what the art schools are doing, seeing what is in the galleries. And from there, I start painting. I just came with one painting with me. But after six months I was able to have around thirty-six.

People are lazy, want a studio. They say, "You can't paint in your room." [But] This is what I did.

I didn't have a job, so to get the money I went out in the cold—I came in the spring, 7, March 2013. On the 15 March, I was out with my sketchpad. Sketching. Outside. Sketching things—the buildings, the trees, whatever I was sketching. And there I was able—people come and say, "Oh you're an artist. That's great! Can we have your number?"

They start giving the portrait to do. So I start getting money. And saw I was doing the sketching and everything. So people will stand there and I will do their portrait. In five minutes, ten minutes. Two dollar[s], five dollar[s], I start getting it.

From there, I went to downtown at the library—the Hartford Public Library in downtown—because it was a cultural center for me. I went there to see the possibilities for an artist and everything. And they found out I was good. So in two months after, I do a workshop for kids with them. And they paid me a little bit of money. So all those things together . . . I was able to start paying my things and build my portfolio.

Here in America, they will tell you,"Oh. no. Your diploma . . . we don't recognize your diploma."

But in Africa, I was teaching artists! I was making them be artists. And some of them are running in the world and having exhibitions and every-thing. And when you come here and they will tell you, "No. We don't know, because you didn't go to school in America."

It's frustrating. It's frustrating . . .

Sometimes I say I am not happy being here because my value is not appreciated.

I used to say to people, "When you come to America, you can be a great person if you want, and you can be a lower person if you want. It all depends on you. Sometimes you have to forget a little bit of the past. But this past has to be your backbone. To support you. Don't forget who you are. What you went through is the experience of your life. So this experience can't be sold."

AT THE SAME TIME, I WAS SAYING THAT I'M AN INTELLECTUAL; YOU CAN'T SHUT THE MOUTH OF AN INTELLECTUAL OR THE BRAIN OF AN INTELLECTUAL. IT'S NOT POSSIBLE. SO I MAKE A STRATEGY OF HOW TO COME OUT.

I CAME TO GET A BETTER LIFE . . .

"I CROSS THE LINE"

José Palacio
Colombia

I came to get a better life, more economic, and to support my family.

My father got a store, a mini store. I work over there with him. But he decides to sell the store, and I find myself doing nothing. I finished my high school, but I didn't do anything more. I got some family over here.

I cross the line, go to find a visa, to fly to Guatemala. Guatemala to Mexico, and Mexico to the United States. We hire a *coyote*. From Guatemala we have to hide in cars and houses, and nobody can see us, because if people start talking, then the police will come, take us out. We are about fourteen guys in a van, and all on the floor, one next to the other one. And the guys say, "Keep your heads down, don't even raise your head."

And they bring us to a house full of people, two hundred, three hundred people in a small house. You got to line up for showers, to eat, to everything. They got different houses, but when I came, I saw they got another house where they start sending people. They ask for money, get the tickets, and send out everyone to different places.

My whole trip, I spent about $5000. My brother—older brother—he borrowed me the money and I have to pay him back. My cousin is waiting for me and I stay in his home. He helps me out to find a job. I got five months in my cousin's house; I can't find work for five months. I don't know places,

As a young adult with a wife and two daughters, José Palacio worked at his father's mini store in Columbia. But when his father decided to sell the business, José's employment opportunities dwindled to nothing. He borrowed $5,000 to make his way to the United States, where he hoped to improve his circumstances for his family, which he had left behind. Settling in the Hartford area, José lived in fear of deportation until his employer assisted him in obtaining legal permanent residence. Until quite recently, José worked sixteen hour days to make ends meet; recently able to cut back to just one full-time job, he finally has the time and resources to study English and enjoy some moments of leisure riding his bicycle.

I didn't even go out because I'm scared of the police. And we used to try to keep contact with the people who can speak Spanish. Go to the grocery store, get the things, and that's it. No contact with English speakers.

I'm a little afraid when somebody comes to me and speak English, because I know mine is not so good. Some people try to understand us, but some others, when I say something wrong—"What? What did you say?"— make me scared. I started doing full-time cleaning, and then find another full-time [job] in a factory—doing manufacturing. I worked sixteen hours a day for twenty years. I wake up at five in the morning and go to bed at two o'clock in the morning. Four hours of sleep every day. They offer better

opportunities to people who speak good English, [that] who doesn't speak, they can get better opportunities. We can see that in my work. When I talk to coworkers they say, "Hey, in the library they got classes, English classes, ESL."

And I went over there and I tried to learn and I read a lot but I need to spend more time speaking English.

When I came, I was illegal. And I got to do something: I say, if I keep doing like this, without papers, I'd better go home. Or if I find some help, I fix it, and I can stay. I came here in '99, and I fixed the problem in 2009. My employer helped me to get my papers.

In my country I used to drink a lot, alcohol, and the friends I got is not the best. And if I stay there I am no good, I didn't go anywhere. And over here I got some plans. When I came here I see myself alone and I start thinking, I do something for me. And that's why I start going to the gym several years ago and then find a bicycle, and I start doing it. I like it, and I keep going. And now I got four bikes already! Now I spend my time in that thing.

WHEN I CAME, I WAS ILLEGAL. AND I GOT TO DO SOMETHING: I SAY, IF I KEEP DOING LIKE THIS, WITHOUT PAPERS, I'D BETTER GO HOME. OR IF I FIND SOME HELP, I FIX IT, AND I CAN STAY.

I WANTED TO GO SOMEWHERE ELSE,
SOMEWHERE BETTER THAN IRAQ. SOMEPLACE
I COULD GET MY RIGHTS AS A HUMAN BEING.

"AMERICA IS A DREAMLAND"

Fouad Abbood

Iraq

My name is Fouad Abood. I'm from Iraq. It was a dream to live in America. Like anybody else's dream to live in America and to be successful. So it started like just a dream, and then the dream came true, and now I'm in America.

So I used to live in a province called Wasit. lt was very close to the border of the province of Diyala, which is under the control of ISIS.

ISIS began to cull most of the English teachers there in Diyala province because they speak the language of the infidel. Because they didn't like anybody who speaks English. They didn't like anybody who had any contact with the American Marines.

I worked as an interpreter—a translator—with a British security company.

Most of my friends, they volunteered. They joined the army, volunteered for defending their areas there, their province. I have up to now some friends still fighting ISIS in the borders. Everyday they text me.

I called my friend when he was on the front line. And I talked to him and he was under the firefight. And he was making jokes while he was talking to me. I said, "Hey! Be careful."

And he said, "No, don't worry. I'm OK; I'm undercover."

Fouad Abbood left Iraq in November 2014. He taught English in high schools in Iraq and served as an interpreter with a security firm, making him a target for ISIS [Islamic State of Iraq and Syria]. As ISIS's hold on Iraqi territories continued to expand and come closer and closer to the town where his family still lives, Abbood's life became increasingly endangered. The United States granted him a visa, and Catholic Charities provided support for him to come to Hartford, where he is taking steps to obtain the credentials he needs to be certified in Connecticut as an ESL (English as a second language) teacher.

EVEN MY BROTHERS AND FAMILY—THEY ARE OKAY. BUT
I DIDN'T FEEL THAT I CAN—OR I HAD TO—
STAY LIKE THIS, THERE IN IRAQ.

I didn't like that situation back there in Iraq. My friends—my fellows—they could adapt. But I couldn't live with such chaos situation, such disruptive, corrupted situation.

Even my brothers and family—they are okay. But I didn't feel that I can—or I had to—stay like this, there in Iraq.

I wanted to go somewhere else, somewhere better than Iraq. Someplace I could get my rights as a human being. And I think America is the right place.

And I applied since 2010. I came here in just after four years. I had four meetings at the American Embassy in Baghdad. Two times, three times I went there.

And they asked me for some evidence. Did somebody really threaten me? Did somebody attack me? They just wanted to make sure that I am the real person who sent them the email. They wanted just to make sure that I *am* Fouad Abbood.

They say that now my case is accepted, and now I am allowed to go to the United States.

We'd been like a group. Like about two families from Baghdad. Christian families and Muslims, and some singles—it was me and two others. And then in Jordan we find that there are too many immigrants like from Somalia, so we joined together in the airport. And then we came to America. But then in New Jersey airport we separated. In America, in wide America.

It was just like a shock to come to America from Iraq. But the next day I wake up in the morning I find myself in America in someplace, in an apartment, with some people from Somalia. I jumped from my bed to the street. I didn't know where to go. It was very cold in the morning. It was 6 A.M., and I stayed in the street, waiting. I don't know what I was waiting for but I stayed in the street, just shocked, and I don't know—just watching I saw some faces that I didn't used to see before in my country. That was a bit frightening. But I knew that's not going to last for a long time. That something good will happen. That I'm going to see something different, I'm going to change my place to some better place maybe. And then I did.

At first, the Catholic Charities used to give us like two hundred dollars every month, and they paid for the apartment rent, and they pay the bill, and they did it for two months, three months, and then they put me in a job in New Britain for manufacturer called ICI [Integra-Cast]. It's some manufacturer for making some aluminum parts. I worked there for about one month and a half, and then got laid off. It was a very hard job. I used to wake up at four in the morning and come back at the four in the evening, so almost I spent all the day there.

Last week I helped some people to study English as a second language at the library—some immigrant people.

My goal isn't to work and make fortune and be rich. I am here to study. To pursue my study. To study, to have a master's degree in English. I have planned for everything, but I didn't expect that they were not going to accept my bachelor's degree, like my university degree. First, I have to be evaluated and then I have to complete some courses.

Before, I was a high school teacher and I have two-year experience in teaching at an elementary school. I hope I can find same job like a teacher

MY GOAL ISN'T TO WORK AND MAKE FORTUNE AND BE RICH. I AM HERE TO STUDY. TO PURSUE MY STUDY. TO STUDY, TO HAVE A MASTER'S DEGREE IN ENGLISH.

or tutor here in America. So I am working on that. And I don't know what's going to happen in the future. But I hope finally I will get the job and maybe pursue my study.

Yes, America is a dreamland. You still have to work hard to accomplish your dream.

. . . YOU HAVE TO ALWAYS THINK OF YOURSELF, "YES, THERE'S A POSSIBILITY THAT I CAN DO THIS."

"I CAN DO THIS"

Bryan Torres
El Salvador

I come from El Salvador. I lived there for twelve years. I grew up over there with my grandmother. Due to the social and political problems, economic problems in El Salvador, my mom had to come here when I was only one year and a half. She had to leave me and my two other siblings, which are older than me. She decided to come here in order to provide us with a better future. Five years after she left, she was able to raise enough money in order to bring us back with her, because she missed us so much. I was like . . . six and a half, I think I was, and at that age I didn't remember her. So I actually thought she wasn't my mother; I thought my grandmother was my mother. My brother and sister, they remembered her, and they were so excited to come with her, and I was like, "There's no way I'm gonna go."

I was very young to make such a huge decision, but my mother, she didn't want me to be unhappy. She knew how hard the traveling from El Salvador to the United States is by land. So they decided to leave me there with my grandmother, and my two siblings came to reunite with her.

When I was twelve, there was two earthquakes that happened in El Salvador, and they were in 2001, one month apart from each other. And that was really traumatizing for me, to like see how the houses just were torn apart, hearing in the news how like some houses are just—fell down,

Bryan Torres was a toddler when his mother left him in El Salvador while she found work in this country. Raised by his grandmother, Bryan was finally reunited with his mother and siblings after a harrowing experience sneaking into the United States with strangers at the age of twelve. Although a strong student in El Salvador, Bryan saw his grades slip dramatically in the United States as he struggled to learn a new language. Between dropping grades and his lack of documentation, Bryan had all but given up hope to attend college when he received some timely encouragement. Now a student at Amherst College, Bryan is one of the organizers of Amherst's Out of the Shadows march.

and like people just died. And I was really traumatized, so I start seeing a psychologist. And the psychologist helped me understand that the reasons why my mother left, and she helped me like understand the life struggles. And then that's when I was able to like connect with my mother, and like I would talk to her on the phone.

My grandmother was going to come here to the United States, because she was getting in the process of getting her green card, and I was afraid that she was gonna leave me again, and that it was gonna be another person leaving in my life. So I told, I called my mother, "I think it's time for me to go and reunite with you guys." That's when I left El Salvador.

The whole trip took about three weeks. And it wasn't legal for me to come here, but I just thought that's what people had to do to come to the United States, just come by land. And like, it was very, very difficult. Like traveling through Guatemala, through Mexico, crossing like all the small towns, all the cities. We had a guide, a person that was guiding us. I remember we were on the border in Mexico, we had to learn how to speak like a Mexican when we were there, because in order to pass and not get caught.

We just kept going from car to car, from bus to bus. I remember we had to stay in one part of Mexico for a week because there was nobody to guide us, so we stayed at some person's house. It was scary, because sometimes we would travel like in a car for twenty-four hours, and then we would get into places that, I don't even know like if they were safe or not. You don't know what's gonna happen to you tomorrow. And being twelve years old, there's a lot of changes happening to you, like just mentally and like even physically, that it's difficult.

After a few weeks of traveling, we finally made it to southern Texas border. They took us to a river that we had to cross, and they told us all, "You made it to the United States, now just go, and maybe they'll catch you, but you are in the mainland so they can't deport you, because you're a kid," or something, that's what they said. It was only the underage people that they did that with, and some people that went with them, and we were like, "We don't even know how to speak English."

We cross the river, we run into, it was a golf course. We changed our clothes, we left our old clothes behind, and started walking in the middle of that golf course. And like there were some people, like dressed very, really, really nice, like rich people playing golf, that were just looking at us like, "What are they doing?" And we just kind of like smiled to them, and then we just started walking. We got out of the golf course, and that's when this truck stop us. And that was the immigration officers that had caught us. And they were like, "Uh, what are you guys doing?" The only thing I knew how to say was like, "I am from El Salvador." And that's what [I] said to them, "Oh, I am from El Salvador." And then they try speaking English and we were like. "No, like, *no comprende. No sabemos.*" And then, "Then you guys have to come with us"— they spoke Spanish, too.

And they brought us into these small, like jail-looking places, and they interview us. They ask us where we were going, they us ask us the infor-mation of our family in the United States, and they actually contacted my mother, and my mother was really scared because she didn't know what was happening to me, and they were really, like rude. Like they were screaming at me, and they were like being very, very mean. It's almost like dehumanizing, the way they treat you. They talk down on you, and like that's where I like started crying, and I told them that I had like a panic attack. I kept crying because I was so scared.

In Texas, it was difficult to like even buy a bus ticket, since we didn't even speak English. So we had people, like helping us, there was people

AFTER A FEW WEEKS OF TRAVELING, WE FINALLY MADE IT TO SOUTHERN TEXAS BORDER. THEY TOOK US TO A RIVER THAT WE HAD TO CROSS, AND THEY TOLD US ALL, "YOU MADE IT TO THE UNITED STATES, NOW JUST GO, AND MAYBE THEY'LL CATCH YOU, BUT YOU ARE IN THE MAINLAND SO THEY CAN'T DEPORT YOU, BECAUSE YOU'RE A KID."

that gave us food. I crossed from Texas to Los Angeles, and we passed Arizona. There were some times that they would stop the bus and they would ask for documents. I was like, "I don't have any documents." I just showed them the papers that the immigration officers told me to show them.

When I finally made it to Los Angeles I was so sick and tired of traveling by bus. It had been like three weeks of not knowing what was going to happen. And like when I got off the bus, I finally like met my mother. And that was really, really a beautiful moment, because I didn't remember seeing her in person, so I just jumped on her and hugged her, and like we both started crying. And then we took a flight to Massachusetts, and that's where I reunited with my brother and my sister.

I was put in seventh grade, and the first day that my mother dropped me off, I was really, really nervous because I didn't really know what was gonna happen. I remember entering the school and like everybody was speaking English, everybody was talking to people, and like I tried to speak to people and like they couldn't understand me. The only person that spoke Spanish was two other kids from my grade, one teacher, and it was just very, very difficult trying to learn this school, trying to learn math, trying to learn social studies, trying to learn science. . . . It was just so difficult to be like in the middle of like a group of people that don't really know your language. You don't really know what to do. I used to carry like a little translator with me at all times. Sometimes when I read books, I used to translate word by word, like trying to learn as quickly as possible, so that I could like talk to people and like learn what I was supposed to learn. And get good grades, because that was one of the most-shocking, saddest moments of me immigrating here, when I like started getting like bad grades, my first year that I was here: I had like Cs, Ds; I had really, really bad grades. To me that was really bad grades, because in El Salvador I was always among like the top students, and then I get here and like I was just doing bad, I was just like, "Oh my God, how am I gonna solve this problem?"

The first and second year of high school, even though it was easier for me to understand the English, I didn't try as hard, I focused more on like working, and didn't really care about school, because I knew I wasn't gonna go to college. It wasn't until senior year of high school that I saw like everybody was so excited about going off to college, going to these like so prestigious universities, and I was like, "I wish I could do that, and I wish I could go to college." I started doing research and I was like, "Actually, if I go to like a community college and then maybe I can transfer to a four-year school, that would actually give me financial aid even if I am undocumented."

And that's where I like took all my money savings, and right after high school I signed up for classes at Holyoke Community College. Even though I had to pay out-of-state tuition, like I was working two jobs, going to school full-time, and paying for my own education, and that was, that was really challenging, like sometimes you don't have time to focus on your home-work and focus on your work. And also, because I was undocumented, I couldn't drive. So getting from Florence to Holyoke Community College was always one of the biggest struggle[s], like sometimes I had to walk two miles to get to the bus stop, because that was the closest bus stop, then take two buses that would take two hours.

Because I was paying for my own education, that's where I started caring more about getting good grades, trying really hard, working really hard, learning as much as I could. And my first semester at Holyoke Community College, I saw this flyer on the wall that said "Interested in transferring to . . ." and there were a bunch of colleges listed. It was like UMass-Amherst, Amherst College, Hampshire College, Smith, Mount Holyoke, Cornell. . . . There was like a lot of different names of colleges, and then they said, "Go visit this person at this time," which, it was Irma Medina, who after I went to visit her, she was like, "Oh yeah," like, "A student just got into Amherst College last semester, so you could definitely do it." And that's where I like start working extra hard to get those grades, to take more classes, and to become like a qualifying applicant for Amherst College or Hampshire College. Because that's where I wanted to go, because like I knew those colleges would offer financial aid for documented or DACA student[s].

For those who are coming here, one of the things I recommend for them not to like internalize any type of discrimination that they face. Because the more you internalize discrimination, and the more you like close your possibilities, those people that think, "Just because I'm undocumented, I can't do this, I can't do that; I won't be able to this, I won't be able to that. . . ." No: you have to always think of yourself, "Yes, there's a possibility that I can do this." Even if it's something that like, you consider something very like, difficult to get or obtain. It's all about like fighting for your dreams in order to like make them a reality.

"THEY CALL US 'BARREL CHILDREN'"

Kamika Bennett

Jamaica

In the 1990s, people in my family started to move to the U.S. There's been a long tradition of Jamaicans moving to the U.S., so for maybe a hundred years there's been relocation from Jamaica to the United States. And my family was just one more family that relocated to the United States.

My mother wasn't the first to come. I remember when I was growing up in Jamaica, I understood that I had many family members who lived in the United States, and during Christmas times, holiday times, they would come visit.

In terms of immigration, there is still, I think, an old motto that's assumed that people move and no one ever returns, or the relationship between two nations and the ways that the immigrant relates to the home country and the new country is . . . there's a severance, but in many cases there aren't.

That's basically what happened to my family. So people came, and then they would come back every holiday, and new people would leave Jamaica and then they would come every holiday. So there was definitely that back and forth.

When my mother came to the United States, me and my other siblings stayed in Jamaica with our maternal grandmother and so we were raised

Kamika Bennett had not seen her mother since she was two when, at age ten, she traveled to the United States to reunite with her. Kamika came from a small town in Jamaica, where her family had lived since the age of slavery. Her mother left her two young children in the care of their grandmother to provide her extended family with better financial support from the United States. Bennett is a student in immigration studies at Hampshire College.

there for those years while my mom was away working in the United States. I knew that my parent was away, I knew that my parent was working hard for me, and I realized that because every single holiday I got the biggest presents!

We weren't wealthy in Jamaica, but I saw everyday even at that early age the material benefits in terms of having family away, including my parent.

They tend to call us "barrel children." There's even like a phrase for it—my case is not exceptional. There's these barrels that people often pack and they send material goods back to Jamaica, and so I have a lot of family members here whose status was . . . basically they had a legalized status, so they were able to go back and forth.

There's a way in which the immediate family got severed from our family in Jamaica but also—me and my sister—gained in a different way because [of] our family that was up here, who would go back and forth, we were now living in the same country.

And then they were, in some ways they were a middle—a middle unit to the family that was still in Jamaica. So whenever they would go back and forth they would come back and provide us whatever cake my grandma made me. So it was a lot more complicated than I think people tend to understand

It might very well be less about the imaginary of a nation that you're leaving behind and a lot more about the people in your lives.

There was definitely a sense of
being impoverished here that I did
not feel in Jamaica. So I'm living in
a very, very wealthy country, and
to feel that impoverished status
weighed heavily on me as a child,
versus basically living in a Third
World country and just going
around. I have all these people in my
family who are in the U.S. and they
get me everything I want, and my
grandma loves me, and all my uncles
are coming this Christmas, and my
cousins are over there. Like it was a
very different feeling to be here

So I'm from New Jersey, having
a backyard. Basically having like a
house, compared to coming here and
living in an apartment. I remember
once my mom would tell me, don't
go outside because people steal
children here and I was just like
what?! What is this country?!!

. . . SO IT WAS A LOT MORE COMPLICATED THAN I THINK PEOPLE TEND TO UNDERSTAND. IT MIGHT VERY WELL BE LESS ABOUT THE IMAGINARY OF A NATION THAT YOU'RE LEAVING BEHIND AND A LOT MORE ABOUT THE PEOPLE IN YOUR LIVES. THERE WAS DEFINITELY A SENSE OF BEING IMPOVERISHED HERE THAT I DID NOT FEEL IN JAMAICA.

"MOST DIFFICULT WERE SMALL THINGS"

Jozefina Lantz
Slovenia

My father was a survivor of torture, so I grew up in a family where my family, where my father, was very much affected by his experiences. And it was the little things in family that, you know, seep out, and [the] injustice of it all. This was from 1947 to '52. I was born in 1953 on the coast of Montenegro. So, lived there for twelve years, and then my parents moved to Slovenia, which is a northern part, which now is a country. So I grew up there, went to school, and so on. Always loved traveling, a sort of national sport in Slovenia to travel. And I have come to U.S., where I do have an aunt who lives in Chicago with her family to visit and to travel through United States. Have taken three months off just for that, and met my husband in my travels. So we decided that dating across the ocean was not prudent: we were already both mature adults close to thirty, and have decided to get married.

Then my husband followed me to Slovenia because I was determined never to be an immigrant. I thought I would miss my family, and I would miss my ways and my country and all the familiar—my friends, all the familiar things, too much to do that. You know, to just willingly become immigrant. I was not in danger, and in that time nothing was going on in Yugoslavia in a way that you felt that you had to leave.

Jozefina Lantz loves to travel and met her husband while visiting the United States. But she was determined not to become an immigrant, so she and her husband returned to her native Yugoslavia, now known as Slovenia. They were forced to leave, however, when employment for foreigners became scarce as the turmoil there mounted. She works at Ascentria Care Alliance as director of Services for New Americans, a job she has realized in retrospect interests her because her father was a political prisoner in Montenegro.

But that was the beginning of turmoil in Yugoslavia. And in '84, after two years of marriage and living in Slovenia, my husband's visa was revoked, and he was given only three weeks. Unemployment was very high, over 20 percent at that time, I think it was like 24 percent or something. Nobody could employ anybody who is foreign without justifying that they could not find somebody from within the country. So he could not get work for two years. So he promptly wrote to his parents and asked for support. He is from Long Island. Of course they did extend their support, and we then came to Long Island to see whether we can work something out.

We stayed on Long Island for nine months with my in-laws, and then moved to Worcester, which is where his sister lives, and we thought it would be good to have a relative in the start here anew. My daughter at that time was not even a year old yet, so I stayed at home for several months and then started working in various jobs, from home health aide, to work at a homeless shelter, working with mentally disabled people. And finally, after years of that, I started working with Lutheran Social Services at that time, which is where I'm still here. So that's the work part of it. . . .

I had a second child. At the beginning of that was not an easy process. Not only culturally, but also legally, because U.S. government—or Immigration actually—decided not to grant me a visa past the temporary stay for three years. We had [an] attorney who had to take immigration offices to court to force the decision. Finally decision was done, and it was sort of funny thing how that works, because a [immigration] worker who we saw for the final time said, "Well, what's the issue here?" and I said "I don't know, it's . . ." and he said, "There is no issue!" He signed, then we were done.

It's not easy to be an immigrant. Most difficult for me were small things, like going to the store and not finding what I wanted to buy, in the way of either food or other items. I was trying to make a first birthday cake for my daughter, and because the place we were living had cake mixes, but not items I needed to make a cake from a scratch. And I was absolutely desperate, not even realizing that I could just use that!

I think Americans are probably the most friendly people. You can come to the store and people are smiling, and are open to friendship, and easygoing. Americans are very willing to help, and I got to say, much more than people from my own culture. This is sort of ingrained in American culture, to volunteering, to assisting, to helping. That is not so in other places: people don't understand what it is to volunteer—I mean, understand what it is to volunteer, but they are not compelled to do so.

For the Americans who are accepting immigrants in their midst, I really want to say that that's an admirable situation. I absolutely appreciate the goodwill and resources and hard work that goes into that assistance to people who are really needy.

Listen, pay attention [to] what immigrants bring in. And they do bring a lot. Einstein was a refugee, therefore immigrant, so there is a lot brought into the country! So if we can all rally about that and look for the best, that would be the best.

OUR JOURNEY STARTED WITHOUT
ANY DESTINATION.

"WE WANT TO INVEST IN THIS COUNTRY"

Bhuwan Gautam

Bhutan

I came from Bhutan to Nepal in 1992. I became a refugee along with my parents for sixteen years. In 1989, the Royal Government of Bhutan adopted an ethnic-cleansing policy and forced around one-seventh of the total population, who were Nepalese-speaking people who practiced Hinduism and Buddhism, sorry Hinduism, and they were forced to leave the country, and they lived in a refugee camp in Nepal, seeking asylum. Leaving Bhutan, I was very young—I was eight, nine years old. My parents decided to leave in the middle of the night without telling anybody because of the fear of arrest and persecution—even without telling our own siblings—and all I remember is following the steps and footpath of my parents.

Our journey started without any destination. My father had some distant relatives in India that he wanted there, and we spent some days until we found the transportation to get into Nepal. We were dumped into a truck and people were brought from that part of India to a refugee camp in Nepal.

It is very hard living in the camp. Refugee camp huts are just like—when you take camping in this country, what else do you have? You have something to eat in a small camp, you're in a plastic hut. So refugee camps are just like that. There is not enough for drinking water, there is no food

Bhuwan Gautam, a community support specialist at Caring Health Center in Springfield, was a child when his family was forced to flee Bhutan during an ethnic cleansing of Nepali-speaking Hindus. His family escaped on foot, landing eventually at a refugee camp in Nepal. Sixteen years later, he obtained a visa to come live in Springfield, where he was supported by Jewish Family Services of Western Massachusetts. Gautam has worked extensively with refugees and immigrants. He is a past president of the Bhutanese Society of Western Massachusetts, Inc., (www.bswmusa .org) and the managing editor of the website NRB, The Voice of Non-Resident Bhutanese (www.nrbbuhtan.org).

135

supply, no nutrition. It is a desperate situation to live in a camp, because a lot of children die of malnutrition, women die with reproductive health issues, elderly people do not have the chance to check the medical records, no medicine, it is a disaster there.

It was wonderful news that in 2007 the United States government and other countries—European countries, Australia, Canada—they offered to resettle around sixty thousand refugees from Bhutan. As soon as I heard that they made this announcement, I applied. You have to apply there, you have to declare yourself that you want to go to a third-country resettlement program. And I applied along with my parents. UNHCR will process you—

United Nations High Commissioner for Refugees—and after that they will forward it to IOM—International Organization for Migration—and there will be like four, five interviews, and they will basically forward you to the Department of Homeland Security for additional screening. And if they find that, okay, you cleared all kinds of screenings and you are safe to travel.

It was overwhelming at the time because, you know, we were traumatized from back in Bhutan to the camp, and again. We were a little bit scared and worried also, because what is going to be the right answer? We did not have that kind of information. And whether telling that we were arrested or tortured—was the answer going to be good or bad? What would the DHS (Department of Homeland Security) want? We had no idea about it, but we told the truth whatever happened, and we didn't have any problem.

And after eight months after the application we were called for an interview, and it didn't take a long time for me to get here.

Before you come to the United States, they give three days' cultural orientation. They teach how to go to the bathroom, how to use the western-airplane seats. They teach about housing, transportation, and employment. Everything they taught us, everything to make sure that you will be oriented before you come. And after completing that, they would put us on a flight. And I came here. I had no idea where I was going to be living that night. It was the middle of the night, and somebody came to the Bradley International Airport from Jewish Family Services, and she said: "Welcome to the United States. I'm your case-manager working with you. You will have a place to live, we have a Nepali family who is going to be providing food for you tonight, and we will talk more in detail in our office next day."

That felt very great to me, because it was so welcoming. Being a refugee—in a lot of ways it is traumatized and stigmatized: nobody would care for you, nobody would welcome you. Getting that opportunity and welcome, it was touching.

The amount of money I received as a refugee was not sufficient enough for me to have my own apartment. It was only $428 a month, and that is given only for the period of eight months. After six months you have to start paying the IOM loan—the travel loan—so I had to start my life earning money and supporting myself from eight months.

I came in September and October, November, that time was election time also, and getting to know about President Barack Obama, who was running for the election, and all kinds of political things were going on.

Christmas time, people would come. I'd never had the opportunity to see how they celebrate Christmas.

After three months of my arrival, I found an apartment, a three-bedroom apartment where we, everybody could live. It was a family of seven including my brother's child, so we lived there. And when they came there, I made a home for them. They were very surprised, and they said, "Is this our home?" Because we had never lived in that kind of place. We are very happy. In fact, I ask my parents that, would you be able to go back to Nepal, we might buy you land and you will be living there in your retired life? And they say, "No, no, no, we don't want to go. There is no medicine, medical facilities there, there is no peace, there is no security."

I was the fourth [Bhutanese] family when I came in 2008, and now, to date, it is over two thousand [Bhutanese] individuals. They live in three cities: Springfield, West Springfield, and Westfield.

I think that, for my generation, we will continue to take this tradition of collective society. But I can see that my nephew is eight years old; I don't think that he will be able to continue what I've been doing. It will be difficult. But then again, you know, we will try to instill whatever the good things are in our family tradition. We were forgotten refugees from Bhutan, and we have no other hopes than to accept this country. And we want to invest in this country, we want to grow in this country, whatever we do will be for this country, because I became a U.S. citizen, but I will not be allowed to go to Bhutan and do anything, so whatever I do will be for this community, for this country. I can tell that refugee communities have been valuable employees to the hotels and restaurants and local businesses they have started to go on for their bachelor's degrees and master's degrees they have started to open up the business stores in the local community. I think this will be very good for us, very good for everybody. Let us welcome the refugees from all around the world. And thank you, United States.

"THEY DID THEIR BEST TO HELP ME"

Saúl Grullón
Dominican Republic

I wasn't aware of being an immigrant, and the emotional charges that came with it, until I was in eighth grade. I was about to graduate from my middle school, and they needed a baby picture of me, and I had a passport with the only baby picture that my parents had of me, and I cut that picture out of the passport and I showed it to my teacher and everyone—meaning my classmates—they realized that I had the stamp of a permanent resident, so I wasn't legal in the country, and I didn't know what that meant. Terms like "social security" or "permanent residency" never came up when I was at home or at school, so I wasn't really aware of it until the eighth grade. But I realized how important it was having a social security number, my tenth-grade year in high school. I went to a scholar-institute program, and in order to qualify for scholarships they needed my social security number, and that's when I asked my parents, and they told me I didn't have one.

Around my junior year, I became homeless because of my sexual orientation, and I was the only homosexual in the family, so it was . . . odd . . . just the thought of liking other men was absurd. And my mother was a religious zealot and my father was a male chauvinist, and homosexuality didn't really have a role in either of their worldviews.

It got physical!

A native of Santiago, Dominican Republic, Saúl Grullón and his family arrived in New Jersey when he was two. It was only as a middle school student that he accidentally discovered his family was undocumented. Help from a devoted high school guidance counselor motivated Saul to apply for a temporary visa through the Violence Against Women Act (VAWA), a U.S. statute.

141

I started realizing that I didn't have to succumb to my parents' way. I didn't have to live a double life. I read books, I read *Beloved*, read *The Wild Oleander*, and I started, like, identifying myself with like these characters who left their homes for, you know, for certain reasons. And I had to run away at some point because my father was such an aggressive, physical man that—he was so aggressive to the point where I, my life was in danger, basically. Although I was undocumented and I really couldn't go far or do much because they instilled a fear in me that if immigration caught me that I would be deported back to my country, so my actions were very limited. And, you know, luckily I had friends that allowed me to stay with them and they didn't really hesitate taking me in, because they saw bruises and other injuries on me that . . . that compelled them to help me.

I was completely scared because I didn't know that I was not wanted in the United States, that I was undocumented, that I didn't have a right, and being told that I was going to be sent back to a country that I didn't acknowledge was my own because I wasn't raised there.

When I could no longer reside with my friends for fear of having to tell them I was undocumented I had to live in a homeless shelter. So I lived in the Covenant House for a short amount of time.

That was very traumatizing, because there were other homeless that were different. That didn't have any interest in reading books, that didn't want to go to school, that college—whenever they heard the word "college," it meant nothing to them. And, you know, teens that were angry and upset with, with their parents. And, and not having a job and not having a place to stay and having to share a bedroom with twenty-three others. And you know, being so restricted, you know, to behave a certain way. And, you know, because if you didn't follow the rules you were kicked out and you were in the streets, and nobody wanted to be in the streets.

I didn't like that living situation, so I looked for other shelters, and that's when I called one of my high school mentors, I was in a program called Pathways to College and it's a program for—it's like a precollege program—for students who are located in urban settings and don't have much resources, and that could use the guidance of someone who knows about college, and someone that can encourage you and push you to apply to institutions like the one that I'm in, and other institutions that provide full

I WASN'T AWARE OF BEING AN IMMIGRANT, AND THE EMOTIONAL CHARGES THAT CAME WITH IT, UNTIL I WAS IN EIGHTH GRADE.

financial aid regardless of whether you're legal or whether you can afford to attend that school.

I called my mentor, and she had a network of people that were interested in helping me. All of a sudden, people just started contributing to like the rent expenses at the YMCA. And I had my own room, I had a side job with Pathways to College, and they tried their very best to help me, although their commitment was to help me until I graduated high school, and here I was, two years after high school and they were still helping me.

A guidance counselor from my school couldn't believe the situation that I was in, and when they looked at my transcript there was a social security number. And it just so happens that every student, whether they're documented or not, they have a bogus social security number. So they verified whether it was my social security number, and it wasn't. So she did so much research, and she looked into Catholic Charities in Trenton, New Jersey, and, they offered to help me at no cost. And that's how I found out about VAWA and how I could apply for, for a green card.

It was very difficult because they needed evidence of the domestic-violence acts, you know, from individuals that saw my parents hurting me at some point. So I needed at least five letters. And the most-important one was from my sister because she, she grew up with me and she saw too much of it, too much of the violence. And they really needed her testimony.

I told my sister that she had to try her best to remember what happened that night. And she couldn't do it. She said that she can never talk about what happened that night, and then I saw it in her eyes she, she was thinking about it. And then I started thinking about it. And I remember coming back home from Barringer High School with a gay bracelet. And my mother seeing me going to my room. When I came back out of my bedroom, my mom saw my wrist and asked me if she could pray for me. And I got nervous.

I hesitated to move forward and to allow my mom to pray for me, but she said, "Come, my son, I just want to pray for you."

I closed my eyes and I feel my mother's arm around me and she started praying the Hail Mary in Spanish: "*Santa María, Madre de Dios, Santa María, Madre de Dios, Santa María, Madre de Dios, ruega por nosotros, los pecadores . . .*"

[Holy Mary, Mother of Jesus, Holy Mary, Mother of Jesus, Holy Mary, Mother of Jesus, pray for us, sinners]. And then all of a sudden I felt olive oil dripping down from my forehead to my shirt, and I told my mom, "Mom please, please mom, I'm your son, don't do this to me, please."

And she said, "You are not my son, and you are not gay. And if you are gay, then this is what's going to happen to you."

And then all of a sudden my mother turned to the stove, she turned the stove on, lit a piece of paper on fire and threw it on me, and then I yelled "Yanny, I'm on fire, Yanny, please help me, I'm on fire!"

IT WAS VERY DIFFICULT
BECAUSE THEY NEEDED
EVIDENCE OF THE DOMESTIC-
VIOLENCE ACTS, YOU KNOW,
FROM INDIVIDUALS THAT SAW
MY PARENTS HURTING ME
AT SOME POINT. SO I NEEDED
AT LEAST FIVE LETTERS.
AND THE MOST-IMPORTANT
ONE WAS FROM MY SISTER
BECAUSE SHE, SHE GREW
UP WITH ME AND SHE SAW
TOO MUCH OF IT, TOO MUCH
OF THE VIOLENCE. AND

THEY REALLY NEEDED HER
TESTIMONY.

Then all of a sudden my sister just pushes me, and slaps my mother, and tells her, "You are not God, and you are not a good mother. Who do you think you are, trying to take the life of your own child?"

And then all of a sudden my sister turned to the cabinet, she took out a knife, and then she ripped my shirt open, and I freed myself from the fire.

She thought about it. I thought about it. And I told her that she had to do it, that this was the only way I going to become legal.

She said, "Why don't you just marry a woman?"

And I said, "What kind of man would marry a woman, being gay, and lie to her on the most important night of her life?"

And she said, "You're right. I have to sign this."

"AN UNKNOWN FUTURE"

Samer Khaleel

Iraq

My older brother got shot and killed while I was transferring him from the place of the accident; we were trying to take him to the hospital, trying to save him. I personally also got shot—two bullets into the lungs. I stayed in the intensive care unit for three months to receive treatment, which unfortunately also the treatment was not the proper treatment, due to the lack of experience of the physicians in the hospital.

That incident really affected me significantly because I am a person who loves freedom and who loves life, and discovered myself that even while I was receiving treatment, I was not receiving treatment from proper people.

Life is extremely difficult. No person or one should have to give up their principles and beliefs. And we have to give up what we believe in, and we follow what they force us to believe in when it comes to religion and practice and principles.

An unknown future. You don't know what's your future.

I consider myself as a neutral person, that I am not aligned with any of the groups or affiliates back in Iraq. And if you live in that kind of society or community, you have to be biased. Either you have to be with this side against that side or with that side against this side. And I couldn't live that life. I couldn't choose a side against another.

Samer Khaleel fled from Iraq to Syria in 2007 and immediately applied to come to the United States. Living in Syria when war broke out, he reluctantly returned to Iraq, feeling he'd rather die in his homeland than in Syria. He was finally granted permission to come to the United States in the fall of 2014. Living in Springfield, Samer is looking forward to applying for U.S. citizenship.

Photo credit: Peter Chilton
Translator: Mohammed Najeeb

149

WHAT WE CALLED IT IS THE "SECOND DEATH." STAYING IN SYRIA, WE WERE GOING TO DIE, AND WE'RE GOING TO IRAQ, WE'RE GOING TO DIE AS WELL. WE DIDN'T HAVE ANY OPTIONS. THERE'S NO SOLUTIONS.

My house that I was living in was in danger. I couldn't live there any longer. Even the education degree I received is considered at risk.

I was still injured because of the hits I sustained. My only option was to leave Iraq and go to Syria. This was in 2007. My psychological state was not stable, my physical state was not stable. But the life in Syria was still better in 2007.

It was very difficult. We travelled by road, and we were confronted by outlaws, under law criminals that their job was to rob the passengers travelling through that road. So when we're stopped by the outlaws or criminals, when they saw my health condition, my physical condition, they kind of—they were only satisfied to take only our money, but not to harm us—as in physically harm us.

It was terrifying. But this was much better to just take it for ten hours—whatever we went through rather than live in Iraq and have it for your all of your life

Leaving Iraq was my only hope to survive in this life.

I arrived to Syria on August 30. By the second week, about the eleventh of September, I registered with the United Nations trying to come to America. I registered after two weeks.

In 2011—on December 15, to be exact—we had to leave Syria to go back to Iraq. Because the Syrian crisis started in 2011.

What we called it is the "second death." Staying in Syria, we were going to die, and we're going to Iraq, we're going to die as well. We didn't have any options. There's no solutions.

When we crossed the border via ground transportation, going back to Iraq the minute we exit the Syrian border, we sat right there, my mother and I, four to six hours, just sitting, looking at each other, reading each other's mind, just trying to figure out what we were going to do. The final decision we made, we said, "Look, if we're going to die either way, we might as well die at our homeland."

The situation's gotten worse. It's gotten worse. The militia's gotten more powerful. The same people who killed my brother and injured me, now they are officially working for the government. And they are just occupying the whole land.

I decided that I must live. I have to produce, I have to support, I have to get a family. I have to start over.

I stayed in Iraq from 2011 to 2014. And it was a struggle and a battle, not against death, but against life, because death was right there. But we were struggling, we were fighting for life.

So in that period of time, I just want to mention that I got married. The reason I got married is: it was only me, my mother, and my brother, so I wanted somebody to be with my mother. Plus, that will encourage me to give me the will to stay alive and to survive in this life because now I have a family.

I was fortunate that after the first ten months of this marriage, I got [my] first baby and that motivated me more for to keep on fighting to survive, but at the same time, that really scared me for the future of my wife and my child.

I was notified that I have an interview near the American Embassy in Baghdad, and I added my wife and my son to my case. I waited a year after that interview. And then they gave me an appointment date to travel. I left everything behind in Iraq. My car, my furniture, my house, my working, my office. I left everything behind. I was waiting for the moment of travel. That was it!

It was exciting. Life is beautiful; things are beautiful. It's a new life. But there were also some challenges there. But we were helped by Ascentria [Care Alliance]. When it comes to English-language learning and stuff they played a big role in that.

All the challenges, believe it or not, are kind of not considered as challenges because I have the people that I can go to and they can help me.

As for my wife, her life has changed here because of the lifestyle. She does not need to wear a hijab. So she is very comfortable that she does not have to wear hijab or is not forced to wear a hijab.

If you think of life and if you want to succeed and move forward, America is a welcoming country. And it's a symbol of life and future.

"IT'S HARD TO TRANSLATE"

Pranaya Bhatterai
Nepal

My name is Pranaya Bhatterai, which is kind of a simplified name in American version. The way it's pronounced in Nepalese is प्रणय भट्टराई. So we have thirty-six letters in our Nepalese language, versus only twenty-six letters in English, so there are some words that it's hard to translate when it comes to the English language.

I came from Nepal. It's a small, landlocked country right in between China and India. It is gorgeous, from a natural-resource standpoint, from the forest greenery, all the Himalayas, the hills, and also the plains. And if you think about Nepal, it's kind of like a brick divided into three different segments. So you have your Himalayas in the top, and then in the middle you have hills, and in the bottom you have plains, which is also called the food basket of Nepal, where you do a lot of agriculture, you grow food, and then that is distributed throughout Nepal. I grew up in the plains, and although Nepal had most of the highest peaks in the world, I had never seen snow before I came to the United States. So, people think that I came from a really cold place and I'm okay with being really cold, and with all the snow in Connecticut—which I'm not. I grew up in a very hot place.

When I was thirteen, fourteen years old, my parents got a diversity visa. It's also called diversity lottery. It's the visa that the United States of

University of Connecticut student Pranaya Bhattarai was born and raised on the verdant plains of Nepal. His parents, who preceded him here, were among the first Nepalis to come to central Connecticut, settling in West Hartford. Years later, as a teenager, he followed.

153

America issues to Third World countries and to other different countries to bring different diverse populations to the United States. So my mother was the lucky one who got the lottery. And they came here and they were not in a position that they could bring the entire family, so me and my sister were left behind.

Even though you're not doing a white-collar job, the money that you make here, when it goes back to Nepal and translates, including that foreign exchange, it becomes a lot more. So they really wanted a good life for me and my sister, and that's the reason why they came here.

Initially, I was very happy because I thought I was going to come with them. But we all were happy because we knew there was something brighter waiting for us if we'd just get through this whole process. I stayed my first two years—and that was when I was doing my ninth and tenth grade—with my uncle and aunt and cousins, and after that I moved to the capital city because, unlike here, when you graduate from tenth grade you are now going to college. So eleventh and twelfth grade is considered as college in Nepal. So I went to the capital city and stayed there, sometimes in hostels, sometimes with cousins and friends, and got that education for eleventh and twelfth grade. And then I started going to college, too. I finished my twelfth grade and I started going to college in Nepal, through the midway—I think I was done with my third or fourth semester—and I got the opportunity to come to the United States because my parents, once they came here, they petitioned for me and my sister to come here. And my sister is still not here yet, because when they were here my sister got married, and now she has a child and a husband, and when you petition for all of them it takes a little bit more time.

When I came to the United States, I started going to the gas station. I worked there for a few months to save that initial money to come to the college. And going to a four-year university was pretty expensive, plus you needed all the SATs and English tests that I didn't have, and I was not really willing to do that, either, so I started with Capital Community College. And I thought, you know, if I have really bad English, they'll put me in ESL, English as a Second Language, and then eventually I'll go to a four-year college. That was always the dream. As I was going through school in Capital Community College, I heard about the C3 program, which is Capital

... THAT IS THE ASPECT THAT I MISS ABOUT NEPAL. IT NEVER FELT LIKE, "OH MY GOD, WHEN IS THE WEEKEND GOING TO COME HERE." EVEN WHEN I WAS GOING TO SCHOOL, EVEN WHEN I WAS VOLUNTEERING IN DIFFERENT HUMAN RIGHTS ORGANIZATIONS IN NEPAL, I NEVER FELT THAT. EVERY DAY WAS A BRAND NEW DAY, AND I DIDN'T HAVE TO WORRY ABOUT WHEN THE DAY WAS GOING TO END.

Crossroads to Careers, which was in conjunction with Capital Community College, Travelers—that's how it started, and later they involved Central Connecticut [State] University [CCSU] and the University of Connecticut [UConn], so that after you graduated from Capital Community College you had a choice to go either to CCSU or UConn. When you are in that program, you also had the opportunity to go to a year-round intern rotation at Travelers [Insurance]. And one of the things that I thought was really tough for me when I first went to work at Travelers was writing emails. You know, I never wrote emails in my life. So I was always scared about, Did I write too long? Is it too short? Am I being too direct? Are people going to not like it? So I had to think about all that thing. So I was very nervous every time I had to hit that "send" button in that email.

When I came here there was a little bit of cultural shock. Very small things that we take for granted. For instance, being able to get up in the morning and take a hot shower which is inside your apartment. Most of the apartments in Nepal, you rent a room or two and then there's one common bathroom for everybody in the whole building. But here it was different. You know, you have your own laundry, you have your own small kitchen, everything. So small things like that, I felt like, "Wow! This is what it feels like being in a First World country." And then the big highways, gigantic highways, I can't fathom how big the highways are. Everytime I saw one of those things that is very scarce in Nepal, I thought to myself, "Wow! This is really amazing." Having Internet in your own apartment, having electricity that would not go out unless there's a huge storm or event.

But when my parents came here, they were one of the very first Nepalese people who came to the United States. There were a few people, but very, very few. You know, everybody is engaged in their own job. My mother sometimes told me that she used to go grocery shopping when there was knee-deep snow in the road, and people would look at them like, "What are you doing? It's snowing." And they would be in huge layers and layers of clothes and they would walk to the grocery stores and bring groceries back because they didn't have a car, they didn't know how to drive. So they had to struggle way more than what I had to go through.

There were definitely instances that I felt like, Maybe I can't do this. And one example I can give you is driving. I'd never been in the front driver's

158

seat of a car, and my first day in a driving school, I tried to get into the passenger seat, and this guy yelled at me saying, "What are you doing? You're supposed to be in the driver's seat! That's the whole point of taking driving lessons." I didn't even know what "the gas" meant—back in Nepal we called it "accelerator," we didn't call it "gas." And then brake, and then you have steering . . . I knew pretty much nothing about cars or driving. I thought I was never going to pass driving lessons. I failed twice before I finally got my driving license, but I did it.

Sometimes we are very mechanical. You know, you wake up, go to work, come home, you're very tired, you have a dinner, you do the same thing over and over. And I have seen a lot of people waiting for the weekend. That is the aspect that I miss about Nepal. It never felt like, "Oh my God, when is the weekend going to come here." Even when I was going to school, even when I was volunteering in different human rights organizations in Nepal, I never felt that. Every day was a brand new day, and I didn't have to worry about when the day was going to end.

A lot of things that we enjoy here, people will die for it in Third World countries. Even if you grew up in a really affluent society, think about how your forefathers, how your earlier generations, how they struggled to make this country what the country is today. And there are a lot of opportunities in this country. I feel really sad when a lot of people say there is no opportunity. You've got to work hard. You've got to work hard and have the courage that you can do things, and just believe in yourself.

. . . SO I RUN UPSTAIRS, I
REMOVE THE FOREIGN BODY,
AND I FALL IN LOVE.

"I DON'T WANT TO BE A RICH WIDOW"

Alberto "Tito" Gambarini
Argentina

My name is Tito Gambarini. I like to use "Tito" because it's the child name of Alberto. I came from Buenos Aires and I came over to this country by accident. I was planning to, by recommendation of my chief of surgery in Buenos Aires, to go to France and get training in cardiovascular surgery and that was 1957. But the contract that I get in Paris for cardiovascular surgery, I had to wait about one year and a half, almost two years.

One friend who was a cardiologist in Providence, and he said, "Why don't [you] wait that year and a half in United States?" And I believed that in the beginning was a crazy idea, but he say, "You are alone." But I say, "Well, I am in practice with my brother," which is a pediatric surgeon, and I enjoyed it, working in the Department of Surgery in Buenos Aires, in Rawson Hospital. But then I have a second thought, I say, "Why not? I am alone." So I call the cardiologist that was in Providence, and he say, "Sure, come here and stay here for six months, eight months, and I will talk with Leland Jones, who is a thoracic surgeon, so you can assist him for a period of time." It looked to me that there were [opportunities], I can wait that time in the United States. And my problem was that I didn't talk any English. But anyway, doctor convinced—the cardiologist convinced me to come. And I did.

Born in Buenos Aires, Argentina, Alberto "Tito" Gambarini graduated from medical school there and trained as a surgeon. He arrived in the United States in 1958 for what was originally intended to be a short visit to study cardiovascular and thoracic surgery. As fate would have it, he met his future wife on an emergency room call and canceled his plans to study medicine in France. For thirty years, he practiced medicine in Hartford, Connecticut. Seeing the toll that medical practice took on his colleagues, Tito retired as a physician in his mid-sixties to study art at the Rhode Island School of Design. He has taught painting and art history, and frequently presents and lectures on the films of Charlie Chaplin.

So I arrived to Providence in 1958, and I become an assistant to a thoracic surgeon named Leland Jones, and I help him, and we become some sort of friends and he say, "The rest of those year and a half that you have to wait, why don't you go to the Philadelphia? We'll talk with Doctor Thomas O'Neill, who is the chief of surgery in thoracic surgery at Temple University Episcopal Hospital, Rush Hospital." And I did it.

So I came to Philadelphia, and one night I was in the—covering the emergency room. The nurse call me, it was nine o'clock at night, and say, "There is a lady with a foreign body in the eye, and she is from Argentina." So I run upstairs, I remove the foreign body, and I fall in love.

So we dated, we married. Canceled the trip to France: I decide to go to Argentina and try to see if I was able to introduce all the equipment, the new equipment for open heart surgery. The government was a mess with the dictatorship. I have a position in the university for teaching in medical school. I had the position, but I never receive the check because of the problems in Argentina. After one year, I decide to come back.

I did my residency in thoracic surgery, and then I meet Dr. Harold Knight, who has training in Cleveland Clinic, and he offer me to go to Hartford to practice together thoracic and cardiovascular surgery. And Elsa at the same time apply as a professor in Yale University. She was accepted as

YOU ARE VERY LUCKY
TO LIVE IN THIS COUNTRY.
I LIVED IN A COUNTRY
WITH A DICTATORSHIP.
AS A MEDICAL STUDENT,
I WENT TO JAIL A COUPLE
OF TIMES, PROTESTING
THE GOVERNMENT OF THE
DICTATORSHIP.

a student and then as a professor. So she teach in Yale literature, specialty in Latin American literature. And I open my practice with Harold Knight. Harold Knight die at age of fifty-one. There was a lot of stress at that moment in cardiosurgery. We have a lot of mobility and a high mortality doing open heart surgery in those years. I get another two partners, a Japanese and another from Canada, and we continue to practice. Cardiosurgery in those years was very tough. One thing that happened to me, to have this thing that you get your health when you do work such like that—continuous many hour in the hospital, so many time you stay in the intensive care unit. I lost the Japanese from a stroke, and the other guy was suffering too from the stress of surgery.

One night, Elsa say to me, "Tito, retire, go to Rhode Island School of Design. I know that you love art." And I say, "Elsa, we don't have enough." And she say, "Tito, I don't want to be a rich widow."

So I went to Rhode Island School of Design. I was sixty-five, sixty-six. And I went to Rhode Island School of Design, and that was my passion. But in the school of Rhode Island design I learned composition, I learned the handling of color, and so and so, for two, more than two years.

My father immigrated to Argentina like many men to make money. Argentina in that moment, 1910, was a very-rich country. People put money buying salon, left for Europe, and come back in five years, they were rich. My father heard that through a good friend in Milan who was British, convinced him to go to Argentina and make money. So my father study the art of design in Milan and become a professional tailor. And so he decide to come to Buenos Aires. The ship that arrived to Buenos Aires was full of men. So Buenos Aires at that time—1910, 1912—the city was predominant male. So that was my father['s] arrival to Buenos Aires. Because in United States were family arriving to this country, but in Argentina were the men thinking about some money, and then return. My father fall in love with Argentina, and never went back to Italy. Very similar to happen to me here. I love this country.

You are very lucky to live in this country. I lived in a country with a dictatorship. As a medical student, I went to jail a couple of times, protesting the government of the dictatorship. Especially the first one that I have, was when the government expel from the medical school Dr. Houssay. Bernard

Houssay was a Jewish doctor, brilliant physiologist with a Nobel Prize in diabetes. He was a teacher to us, and I became an assistant to the Physiology Department. And the reason that they expel Dr. Houssay was political, and because he was a Jew. We went on strike, two hundred students. We close the building, and the following morning soldiers and policemen come with machine gun and put all of us in jail. At that time, you were unable to talk in a cafe or any place against the government. You were there and then suddenly you talk against the government, immediately you don't know what will happen to you. That is to live in another country.

I love America. I was lucky to have a wife, three children in America.

"NAMES ARE IMPORTANT"

Vira Douangmany Cage

Laos

Names are important when you're a refugee immigrant—when you're an immigrant to this community, to this country. Because you want to blend in, you want to be accepted, you want to make it easier for people to pronounce so they don't mess it up. So there's a lot of politics in names.

I came here to the United States in 1980. We were living in a room in Brookline, Massachusetts. It was a refugee resettlement house. And my parents and my four other siblings shared a mattress in this room in this big house. And I remember being in Brookline and seeing the apple trees in the front yards of people's homes, and I thought that was so great, because I remembered fruit trees in Laos as a child. And it was a new experience of seeing big homes and walking on sidewalks and seeing things that were just enormous in my eyes, and absorbing the new environment that I found myself in.

In Laos, I remember my dad coming home and I would greet him by opening our metal gate, and he would come in with his scooter. And he would pick me up and we would ride into the front yard—I would be with him on his scooter doing that. And he would greet me with a brown paper bag full of whatever fruit he found or bought along the way, and so I looked forward to my dad coming home each afternoon. I remember that we had

Amherst resident Vira Douangmany Cage was four the night her mother told her to be silent lest they be shot crossing the Mekong River from Laos to Thailand. After years of living in squalid conditions as refugees, she and her family obtained visas and landed in Dorchester, Massachusetts, where she experienced repeated episodes of discrimination in elementary school. Vivid memories of both that prejudice and the hardships her family endured as they tried to adapt to American culture inform her present-day advocacy work as an organizer with the American Civil Liberties Union of Massachusetts and a representative on the Amherst School Committee.

I REMEMBER BEING IN THE THAI REFUGEE CAMPS. I REMEMBER MY COUSINS, MY DAD GATHERING ALL OF US AND SAYING THAT WE FINALLY GOT ACCEPTED.

lots of chicken. We had a chicken coop, and each morning I would go check to see if we had any eggs, and I would bring some back to my mom. And I remember in the morning having fried eggs to eat, with the sticky rice and the fish sauce.

And I remember the plane ride to the United States, and I remember the plastic bag that we had—I think it was just one bag, and it had the big letters ICM [Immigrant Case Management] on it. And we carried with us whatever we were able to bring on that plane ride. And I just remember that all of a sudden we had to pack up and prepare to board this plane.

I remember being in the Thai refugee camps. I remember my cousins, my dad gathering all of us and saying that we finally got accepted.

I remember starting kindergarten. I remember those early first, second, third grades of not really understanding that I was picking up a new language: I just was a student, you know, amongst my peers, and I was just listening a lot—being quiet a lot. And part of the reason why I was a quiet child—a quiet person in the classroom—was because I believe my mom impressed upon me the importance of being quiet. And this is when we had journeyed, made our way of escaping Laos.

I remember boarding a bus, a very-crowded bus, and she packed up hot sticky rice in a bamboo container and rice vessel, and I remember the beef jerky, the dried beef jerky that she packed up for us. And it was my mother, it was my little brother who was about two years younger than me at the time, and it was me. And we finally ended up in a remote place, a place I was not familiar with at all. We were at this person's house that lived by a creek or a river, and they made us shampoo using different herbs and natural products and fruit and whatnot, and citrus. And we used it to wash our hair in this creek where we had to walk down, and it just was beautiful to me. And it was a really nice moment of bathing in that water. I remember the water being very clear, I remember the rocks, I remember it being sunny and warm. And then later on that night my mom told me to be quiet, because there were soldiers on the banks of the river, and they had guns and they were ready to shoot if they heard or saw us. I stayed quiet, I didn't cry, and we managed our way across the river. And I remember being dragged, and being told that I was dragged, through lots of thorny bushes before ending up at a safe house. My legs, my mom told me, were all scratched up and bloodied because she had to drag me, and probably carried my little brother.

I believe the next morning I remember my mom holding my hand, and we walked by this lot, and it had soldiers camping and cooking, and my mom nonchalantly said hello as we walked past by them. And she was my— she was the first actress, you know. I knew she was acting, I knew she was playing it cool. Even as a young person, I sensed that.

My dad had a couple of luggages, I think two luggages, when we were at the camps. It contained photos—family photos—and probably other things. And I remember there was a big fire, and he had put the suitcases in a barrel that we used to store water. And the fire just consumed it. We lost a lot of pictures.

So I definitely claim my red, white, and blue stripes. I definitely claim that, especially in places where I get denied that—where that is rejected, or I'm not seen as American enough, or a real American or a true American. I'm talking about racism, I'm talking about xenophobia, I'm talking about being scapegoated. I'm talking about being rejected.

NAMES ARE IMPORTANT WHEN YOU'RE A REFUGEE IMMIGRANT—WHEN YOU'RE AN IMMIGRANT TO THIS COMMUNITY, TO THIS COUNTRY. BECAUSE YOU WANT TO BLEND IN, YOU WANT TO BE ACCEPTED, YOU WANT TO MAKE IT EASIER FOR PEOPLE TO PRONOUNCE SO THEY DON'T MESS IT UP. SO THERE'S A LOT OF POLITICS IN NAMES.

You know, I remember starting first grade, coming off that yellow school bus for the first day in Shawsheen Elementary School, and this kid who was from an older grade comes walking up to me and calls me "Chink" in my ear. And I didn't know what that was or what that word was. And he did it again the following day, and I knew to avoid him by then because it didn't make me feel good, and he was doing it in such a hostile way, and you can sense that as a young child. And that was a white boy, you know. And when I started the rest of my fourth grade in Dorchester at the William E. Russell [school], a black kid did that to me, you know? And it was stunning, it gives you pause. And that was the environment that I grew up in. And sometimes it was about just being safe; sometimes it was avoiding injury and harm, verbal or physical.

And so when you see your neighbor El Salvadoran families and their little kids having to go through the public schools and having to also try to adapt and to blend in and to survive and to succeed and to struggle, it reminds you of your own experience and the hardships your parents faced. When they don't know the language barrier well, and they don't know how to navigate the system very well, and they don't know how to negotiate very well and they're constantly taken advantage of. And so, to see the economic struggle, to see the struggle in school—it inspires me to use what I know in my own experience for education, for awareness. So that's how I'm dealing with my past.

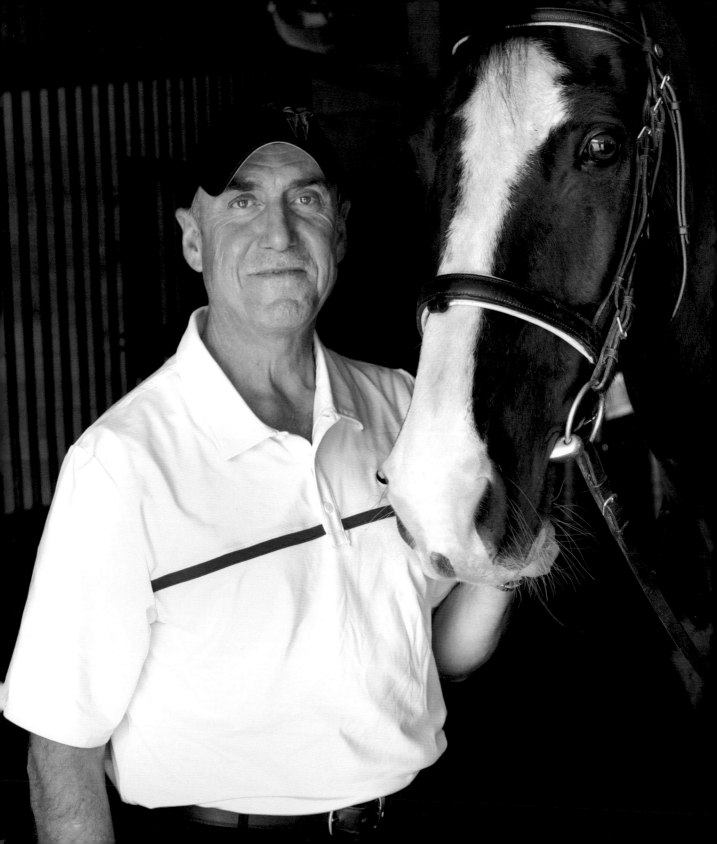

I CAN START OVER

Roger Kasbo

Syria

Syria was the country before the war, around like 2008 or 2007, they put her on one of the four country safest in the world. And when they start the war, it is in the end. There is not safe anymore, because of this war.

I hate war. So, because of the war, I moved here, because I had really good chance from my younger brother [who] used to live here since 1984. And he applied for me for the immigration as a sister and brother, so it took me more than fourteen years to get it. So I got it when exactly start the war. But I was married, and I have two kids, so I tell the counselor I have a family, so they sent for me as a green card immigration for all my family. I had to wait another one year. So when I got it, I moved here.

When the war started, and my city now on the ground, unfortunately. Some cities, still it's safe and everybody work. And we heard about a lot of friends in Damascus working good, and in Hamar, Homs, it's like a lot of cities still nothing. Like Latakia, Tartus—I have my cousin in Tartus and I have my friend in Latakia, and in Damascus there's nothing. But they told me like, "You just move from Aleppo to another city!" I said, "Well, I can start over, so I want to start over." I decide to move here.

For me, I can do it, but for my wife and my kids, it's really hard, because, you know, when you move completely from a different culture to other

Horse-jumping champion Roger Kasbo came to the United States for the first time in 1990. Unable to stay, he returned home to Syria, where he met his wife and fathered two daughters. After a decade of waiting to return to the United States, he got his lucky chance in 2012, just as war was beginning to devastate his beloved city, Aleppo. He lives and works in Shelburne Falls.

culture, try to find friends, try to find
how the people here, you know, treat each
other, and how they deal with each other,
it's not easy. But only the first six months
was hard for me to understand everything, how they do work here. People who
I work with, they are really helpful and
understanding, and they are really kind.
I felt as like I find my second family here.

My graduation, its specialization is
breeding and training and showing
horse jumping. I spent twenty years in a
very good condition and very safe area,
and all my life, you know, I start riding
horses when I was thirteen years old.
Since 1975. So now I become like around
like forty-four years about experience.
I love to be around the horse, and do
such crazy games, like kind of vaulting.
Everybody here, they do it on the circus.
But back home, we do it as like danger-
ous game. Only the really strong people
can do it, and we [are] really proud about
our strongest arm, and do something like
that. I like the jumping more than the
other, and so I continue in the jumping.
I took my first jumping championship
grand prix, show jumping, in Syria 1989,

and also in 1997 I took the second. I had a lot of prizes over there, and then I start to train my team in Aleppo, and then I got really good position as a manager over there and I apply for as course designer for how to build the obstacle in the arena for the show jumping, this is really hard. So I also enjoy in this two years as a course designer. And I help a lot doing kind of job in my country as a volunteer, because, you know, everybody like the horse, he can do a lot of things volunteer, but not in this situation if you don't have any job and you have to really find a job.

I recommend everybody, if he's gonna try to do something, he can do it here in U.S. You just start, you go over. Don't stop. Just move!

FOR ME, I CAN DO IT, BUT FOR MY WIFE AND MY KIDS, IT'S REALLY HARD, BECAUSE, YOU KNOW, WHEN YOU MOVE COMPLETELY FROM A DIFFERENT CULTURE TO OTHER CULTURE, TRY TO FIND FRIENDS, TRY TO FIND HOW THE PEOPLE HERE, YOU KNOW, TREAT EACH OTHER, AND HOW THEY DEAL WITH EACH OTHER, IT'S NOT EASY.

. . . SOMETIMES IT WAS ABOUT JUST BEING SAFE; SOMETIMES IT WAS AVOIDING INJURY AND HAR

OUR JOURNEY STARTED WITHOUT ANY DESTINATION.

. . . YOU HAVE TO ALWAYS THINK OF YOURSELF, "YES, THERE'S A POSSIBILITY THAT I CAN DO THI